Joyful Heart Bunnies and their Easter Eggs Coloring and Activity Book

Coloring Pages, Mazes, Word Searches, and More!

A "Critter Activity Book"
by Julia L. Wright
from HieroGraphics Books.

Published by HieroGraphics Books as part of the "Critters Activity Book" collection created by Julia L. Wright.

For information regarding permissions, write to:
info@hierographicsbooksllc.com

www.hierographicsbooksllc.com
Manitou Springs, CO

Cover Design by Julia L. Wright ©2021

Printed in the United States of America

First Printing, March, 2021

ISBN: 978-1-954955-00-4

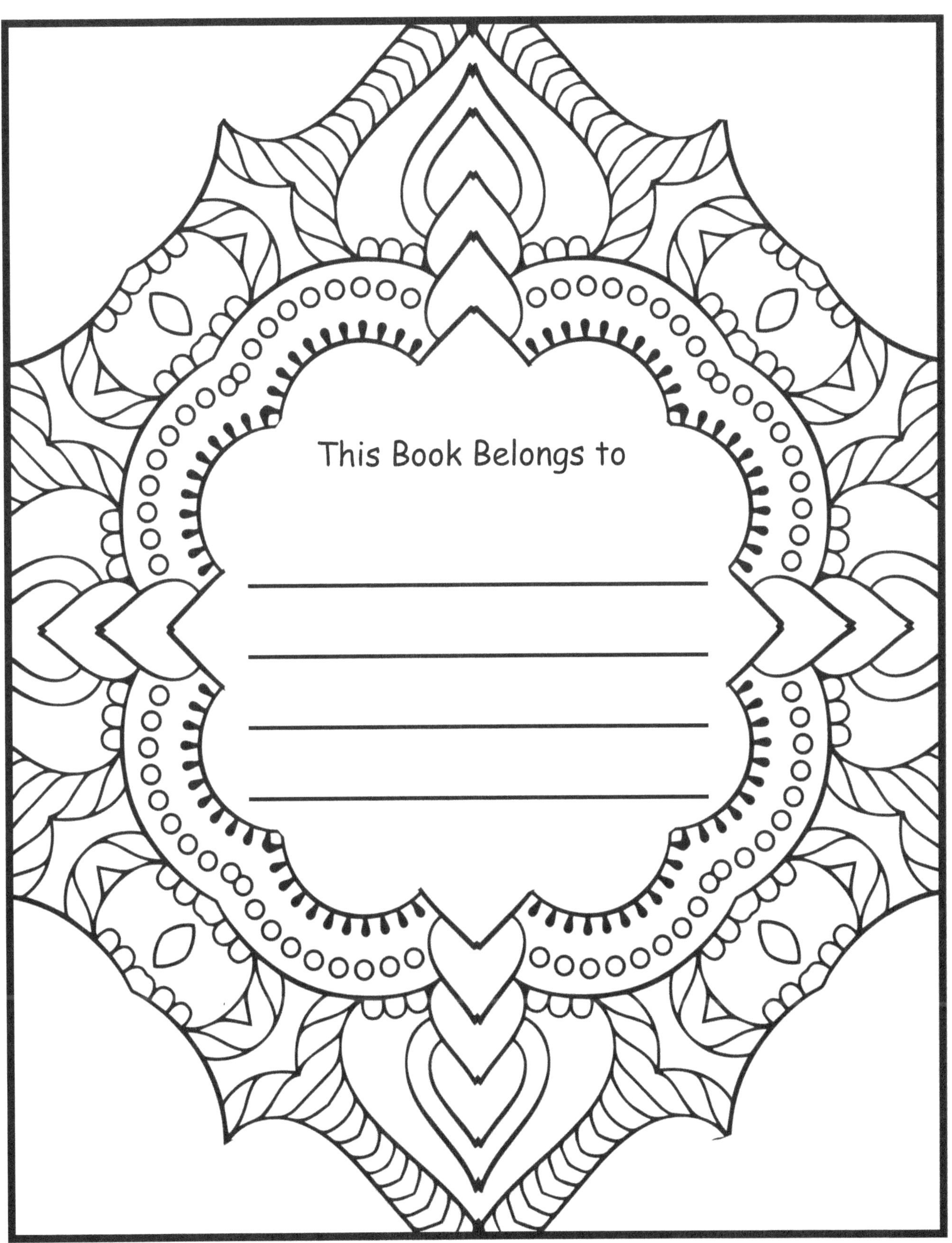
This Book Belongs to

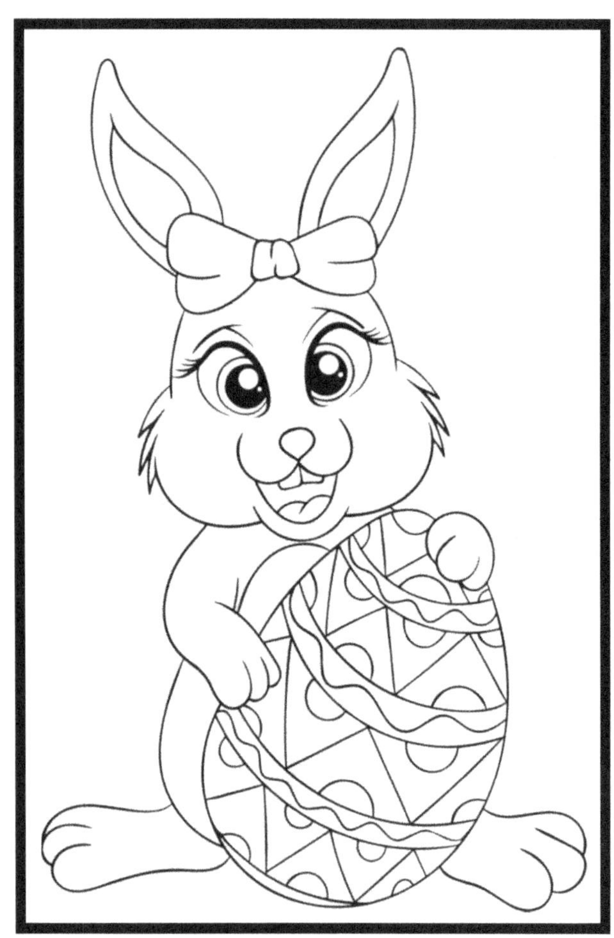

Bettina Bunny would like to tell you a little about what you will find inside this coloring and activity book. She knows you must appreciate bunnies because you bought this book to have some fun by coloring them.

Each of the Bunnies have been given a name. There is a very short story about what they are doing in the fantasy scene on each page.

In this book you will find over a dozen joyful Bunnies engaged in many activities relating to decorated Easter eggs. Some are getting ready to deliver them to a house or painting an egg. There are a half dozen egg-shaped Mazes, six 4x4 cell Sudoku Puzzles, plus three types of Word Puzzles to solve as activities to do beyond coloring these cute Bunnies.

When doing the Word Search Puzzles, you will be circling the words listed above the puzzle found among a random series of letters. Some will be straight across, others will be found on an angle or spelled in a backwards manner.

One Word Search Puzzle is based on the names of the Bunnies in this coloring book. The second Word Search Puzzle has words that relate to what you will color or a name of a Bunny. The last one has words related to things you can color.

The Mazes are egg-shaped and have bunnies needing your help to discover the path to where take to get their egg to put into the basket below. There is just one path that will lead the way they must go to deliver that egg. If you find the Mazes in this activity book challenging, you might want to copy them to work on outside of the book.

The clues for the first Crossword Puzzle will have you fill in the name of the Bunny the clue describes. Clues for the second one are questions that relate to an activity a Bunny is engaged in on one of the pages.

There are a dozen Easter eggs to color with two types of designs inside them. A half dozen Easter eggs have designs based on flowers, the other half dozen Easter eggs have hearts in their designs.

The half dozen 16-cell Sudoku puzzles have easy to draw images of a star, flower, heart and an egg to solve each puzzle.

When coloring, remember these are your images to create and make them look however you like to color. Some have areas of very tiny lines, but you don't have to color in each small section. You may chose that area to be just one color, or color every other one of the tiny sections. This is meant to be a fun activity book, and maybe just a little challenging.

At the end of this book are pages where budding authors can write stories about what their favorite Bunnies are doing. Aspiring artists have a space they can use to sketch an image for that story.

So now it's time to start coloring Bunnies or engaging in some of the activities you will find inside.

HAVE FUN!

What You Will Find On The Pages In This
Joyful Heart Bunnies and their Easter Eggs
Coloring And Activity Book

On Pages 7 to 17 you can color joyful bunnies carrying baskets of eggs along a path.

On Pages 19 to 29 have egg-shaped Mazes to solve to guide a bunny on a path to take a decorated egg to a basket below.

Page 31 has an Easter basket filled with six big patterned eggs to color.

On Pages 33 to 43 you can color a joyful bunny in different scenes and some large decorated Easter eggs.

Page 45 has a Word Search Puzzle using the names of the bunnies.

Page 47 has a Word Search of a mix of the names some bunnies and glossary words used in the stories.

Page 49 has a Word Search for words relating to activities you can do or what you will be coloring.

On Pages 51 to 61 there are a half dozen eggs filled with heart-based designs to color.

Page 62 has clues for a Crossword Puzzle that needs you to name the bunny that fits the description of an action in the clue.

Page 64 has clues for a Crossword Puzzle relating to something you can color or what a bunny is doing in one of the scenes.

On Pages 67 to 77 there are a six Easter eggs filled with flowery designs to color.

On Pages 79 to 89 there are Sudoku Puzzles with images of eggs, hearts, flowers and stars to place in 4x4 box to solve the puzzle.

Pages 92 to 107 have the solutions for the bunny Mazes.

Page 100 has the solution for the Bunny Names Word Search on page 45.

Page 101 has the solution for the Bunny Names and Glossary Word Search on page 47.

Page 103 has the solution for the Word Search on page 49 relating to activities you can do or what you will be coloring.

Page 105 has the answers for the Bunny Names Crossword Puzzle on page 63.

Page 107 has the answers for the Bunny Glossary Crossword Puzzle on page 65.

Pages 108 to 113 have the answers for the Sudoku Puzzles.

On Pages 114 and 115 there are some book suggestions that kids who love wild animals and Nature might enjoy.

Pages 117, 119, 121, 123, 125 and 127 offers places for budding writers to "Write a Story" about their favorite bunny they found in this book.

Pages 116, 118, 120, 122, 124 and 126 have spaces for aspiring artists to draw images relating to the story they wrote or create a new illustration of a bunny in a different environment.

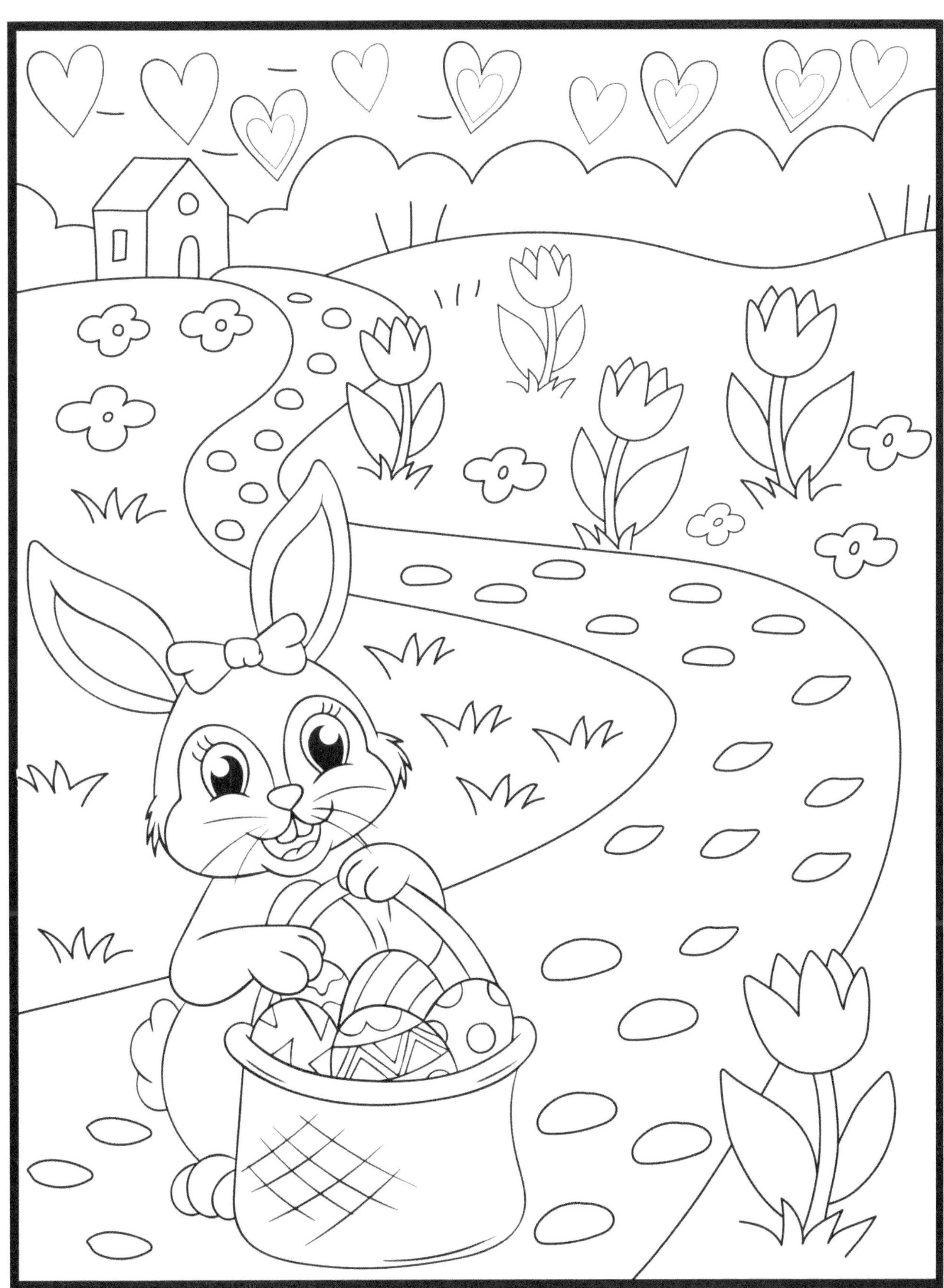

Briannah is walking through a field of tulips with a basket of Easter eggs on a path leading up a hill where hearts are joyfully dancing in the sky to welcome her home.

Scruffy has a basket on his back filled with Easter eggs and is excited to see more eggs hanging on a tree to gather and add to his collection of eggs to bring to his friends.

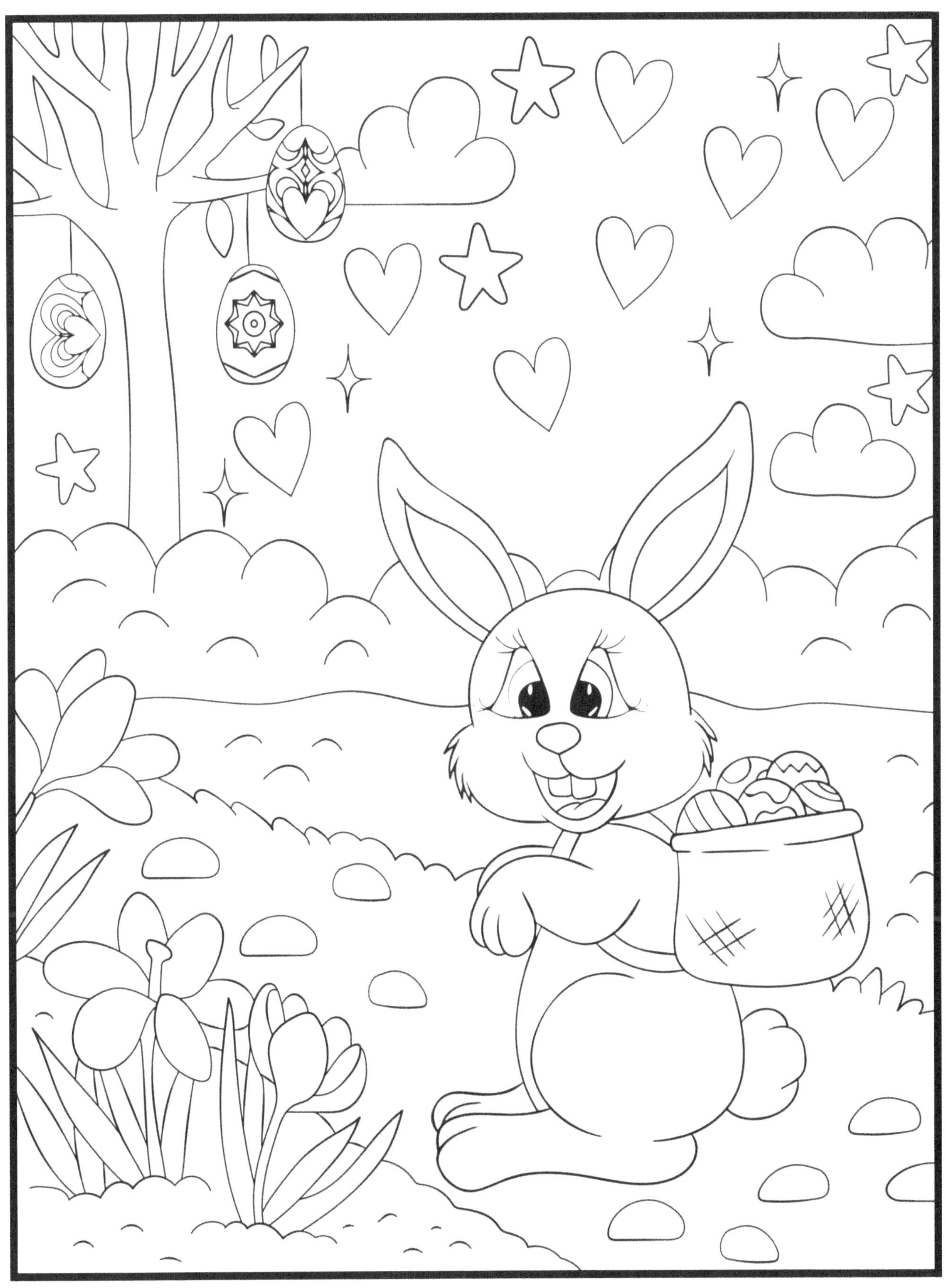

The sky above **Blythe** is filled with stars and hearts. Big flowers are making her smile as she prepares to carry her basket of Easter eggs along the path to her forest home.

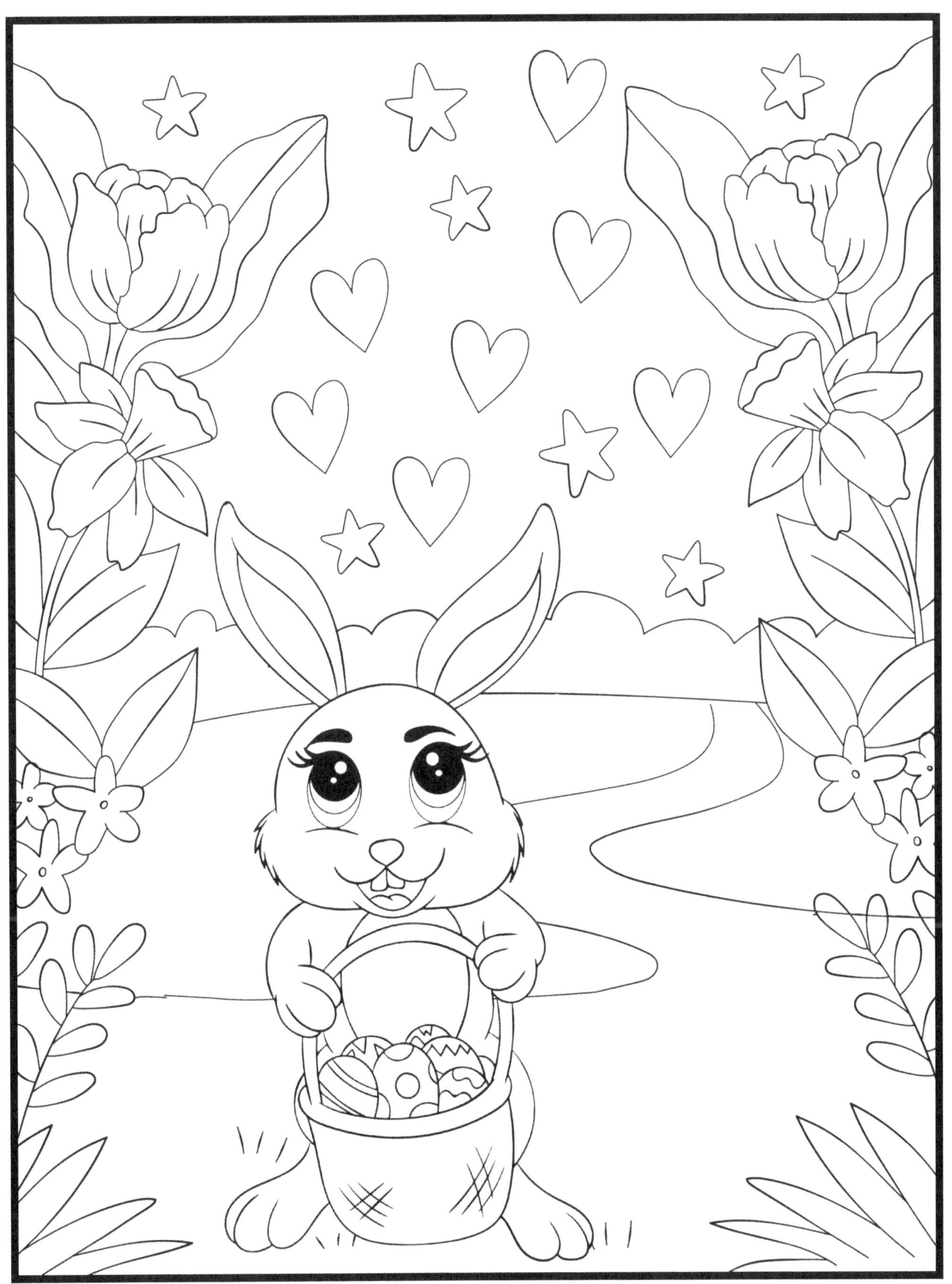

Beaufort is smiling as he admires the tulips blooming around him while resting a basket of colored eggs on a moss covered stump before he brings them home to hide for his children.

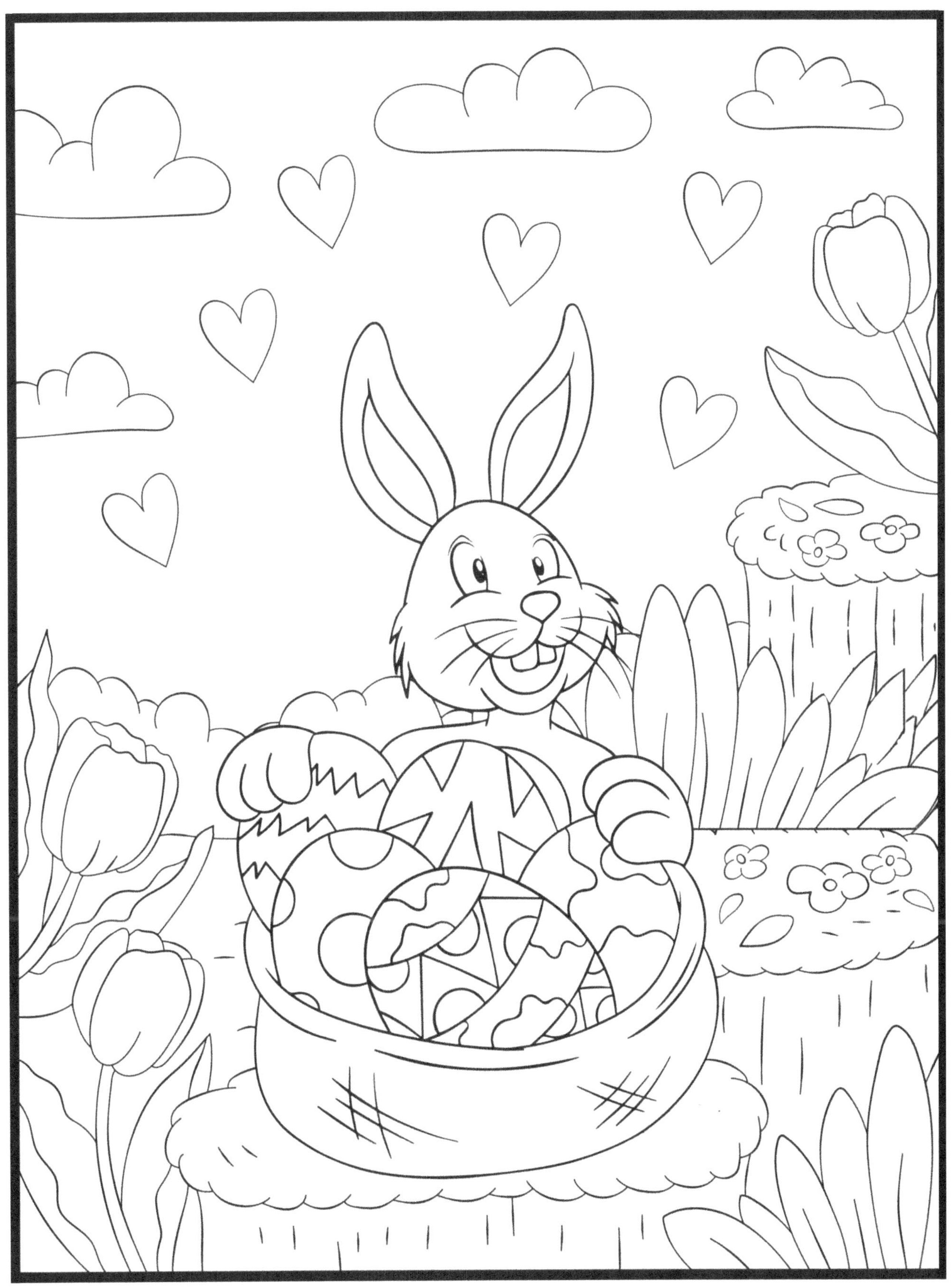

Love fills the air as **Whiskas** begins to walk through a yard filled with tulips and small flowers to bring her basket of Easter eggs to a neighbor's family in the nearby cottage.

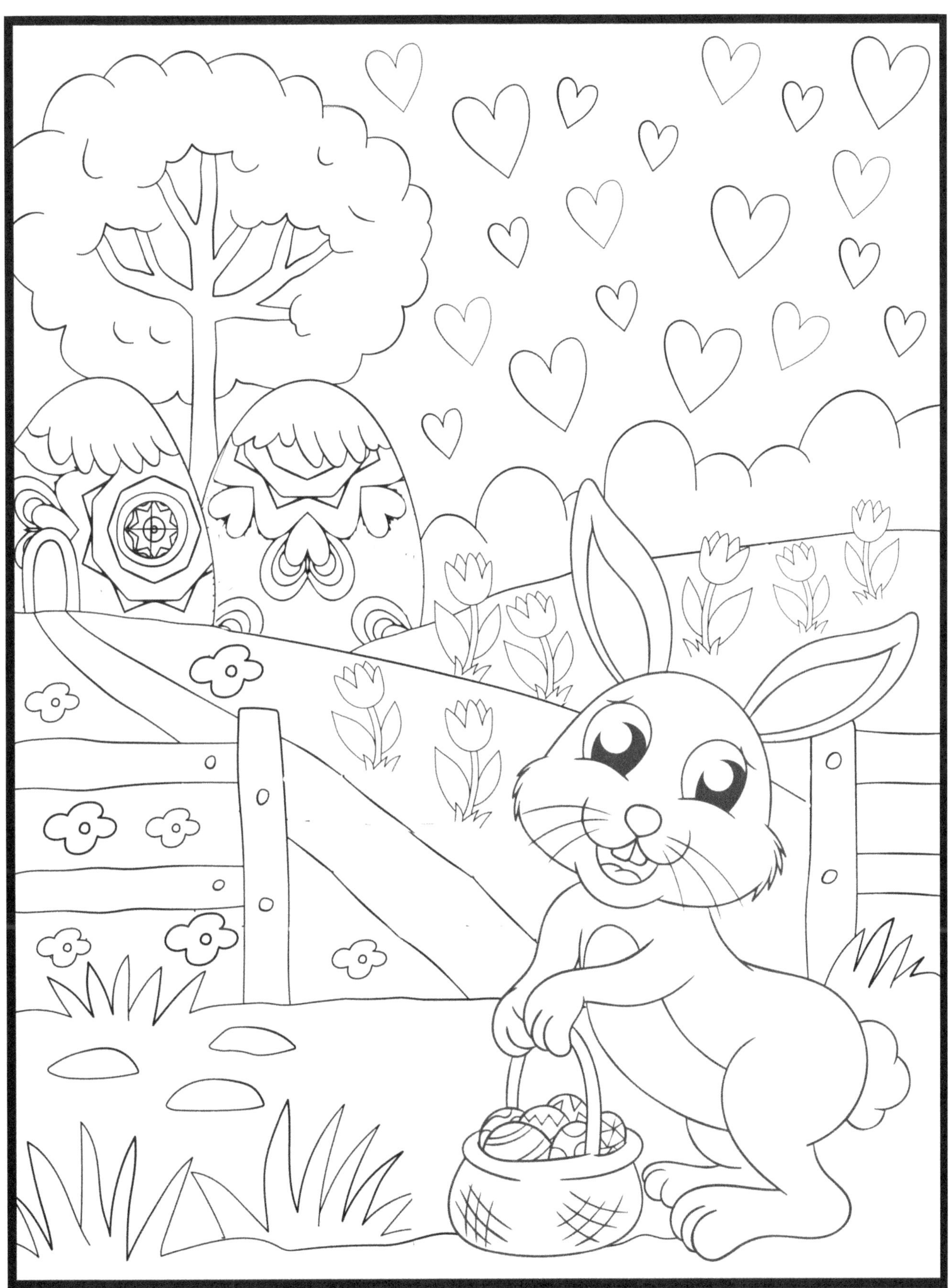

Twinkling stars and hearts fill the air as **Hairbrain** looks for more Easter eggs among the flowers and grass to add to his basket to bring home and hide for his children to find.

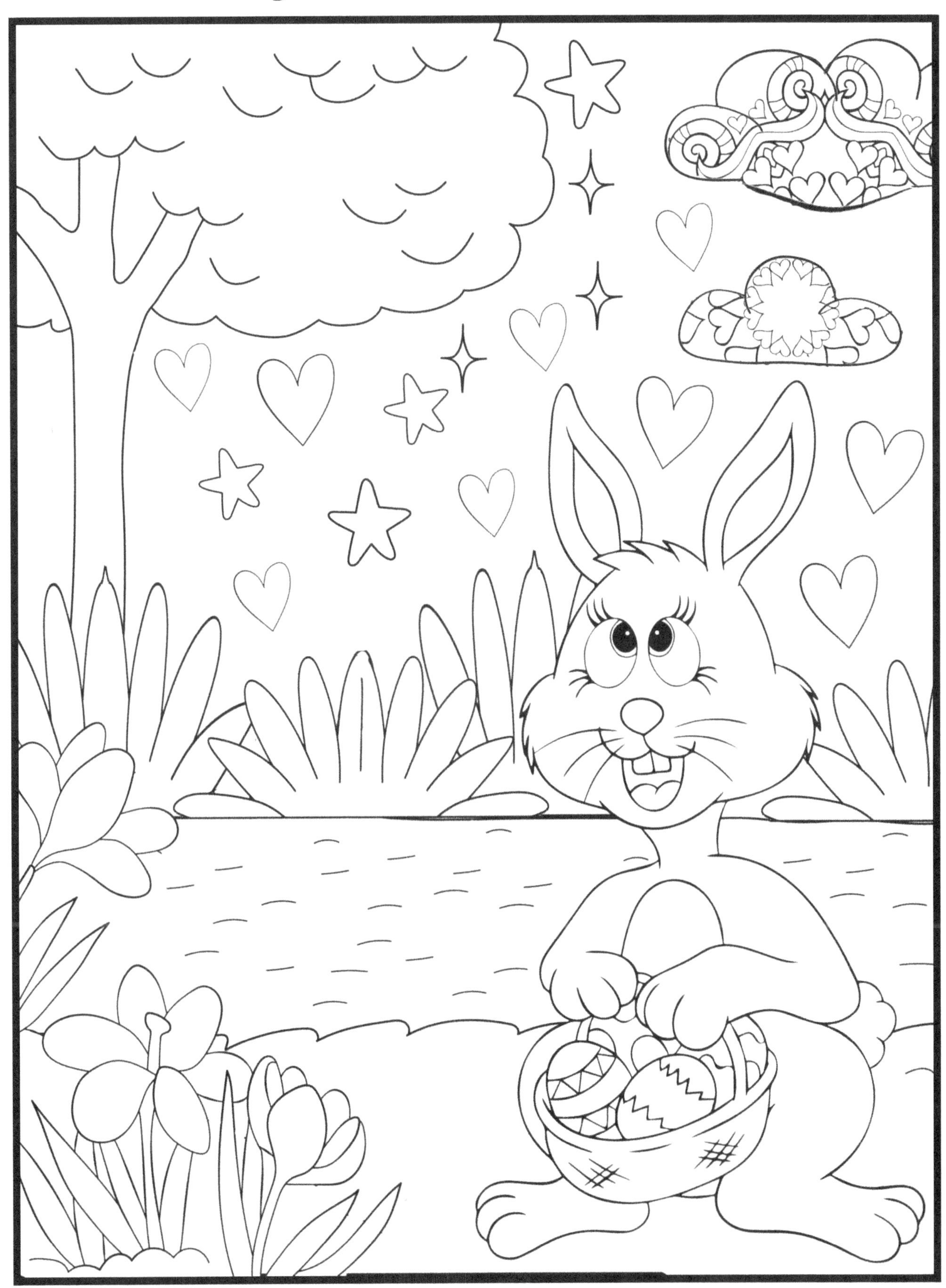

Bigfoote needs your help to find the path to follow
to place this first egg in an empty Easter basket.

You can find the Solution to Bigfoote's maze on page 92.

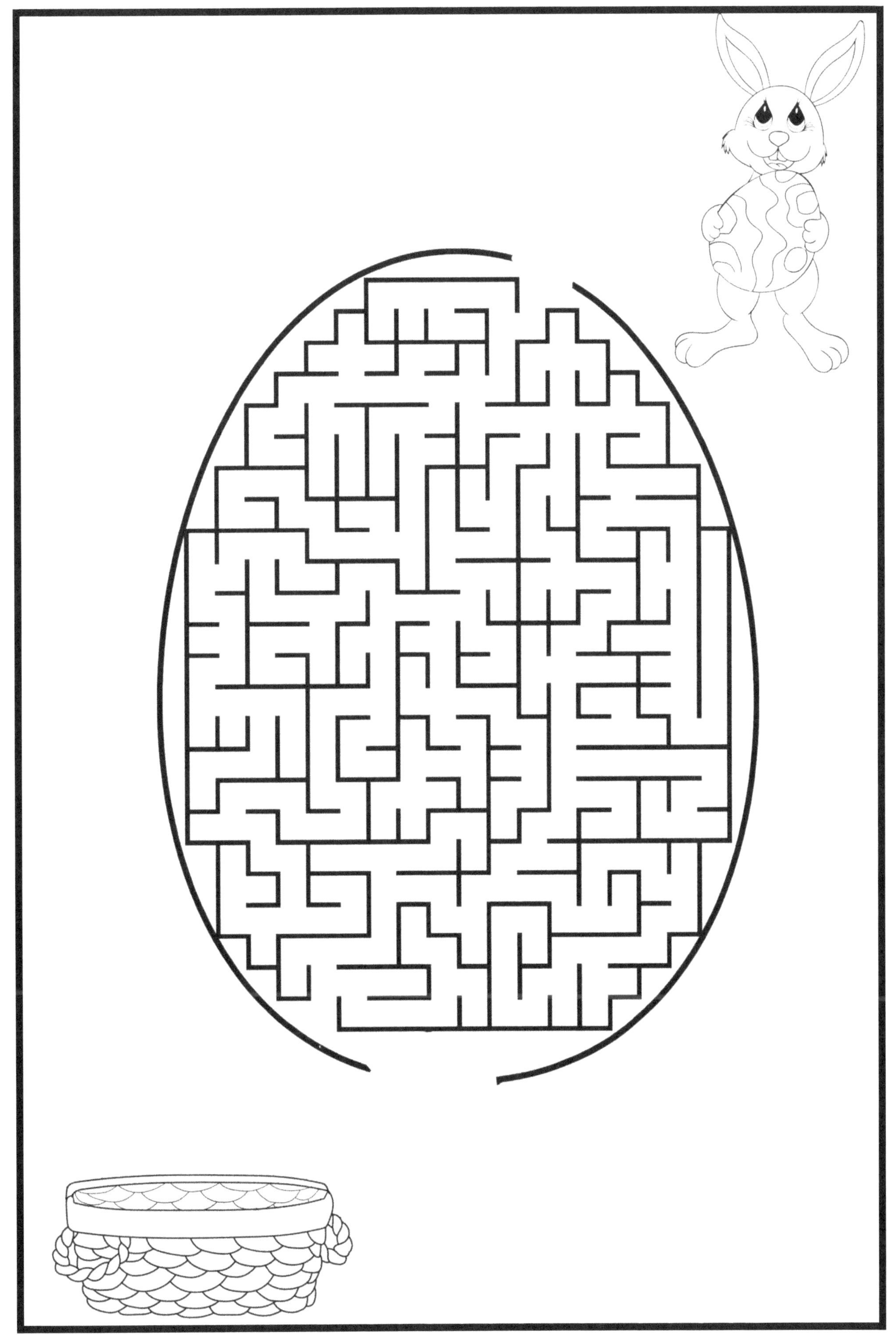

Yoda would like to have your help to find the way to travel to place his egg next to the single one in the Easter basket.

You can find the Solution to Yoda's maze on page 93.

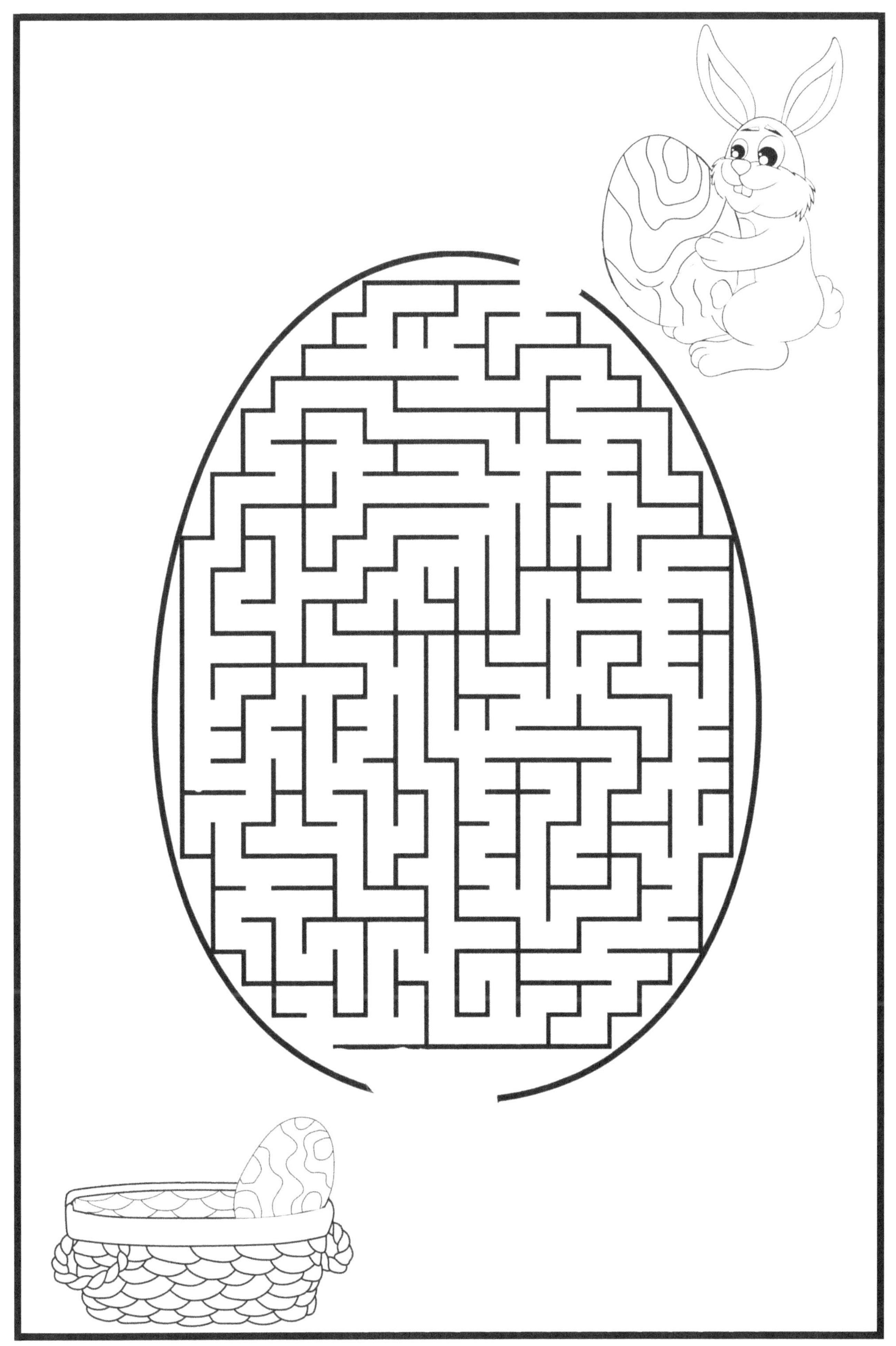

Delicata is asking for your help to find the fastest path to place another egg into the Easter basket with a couple of eggs.

You can find the Solution to Delicata's maze on page 94.

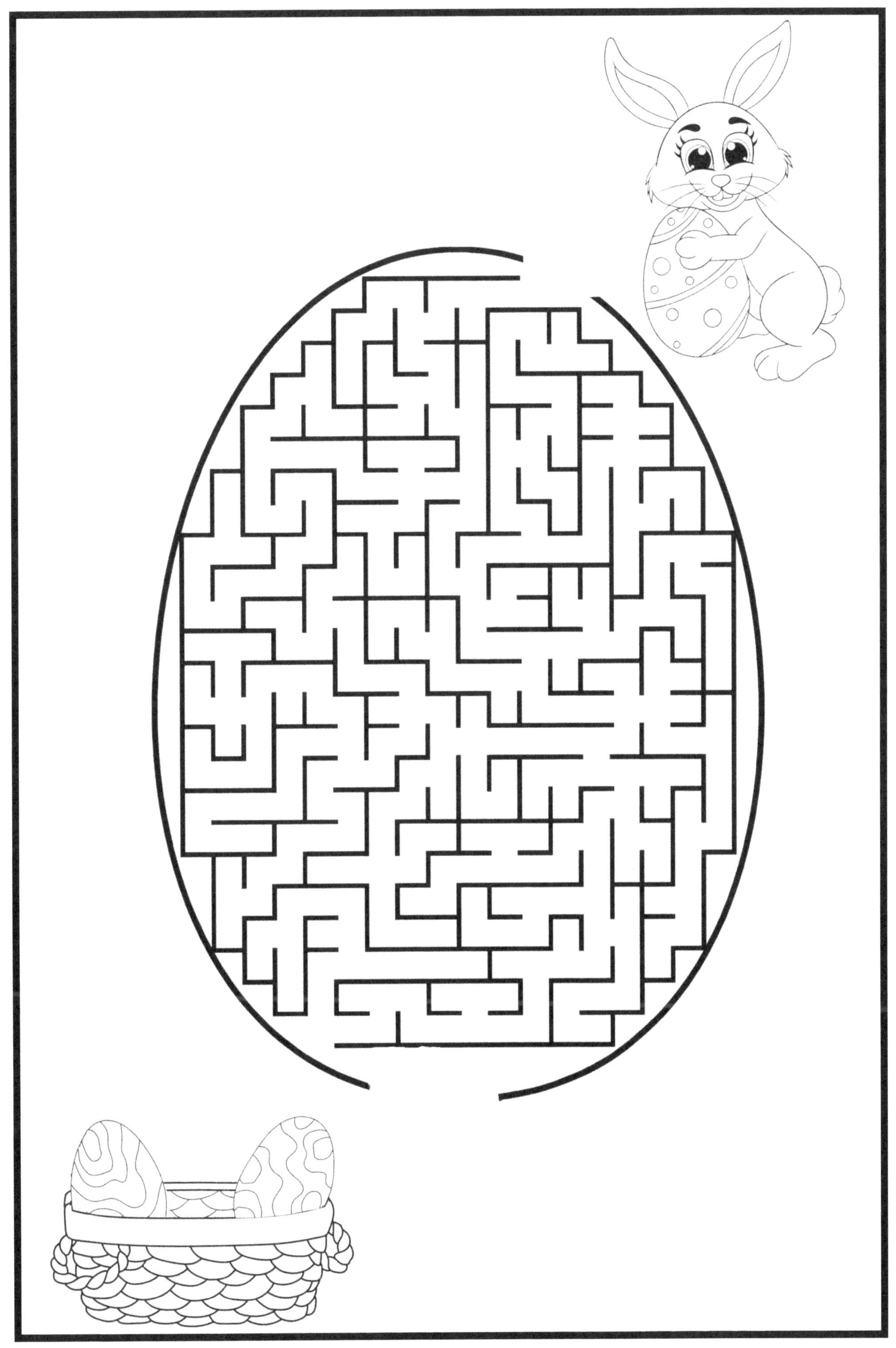

Bettina wants to ask for your help to find the path to place her egg into the Easter basket quickly filling up with eggs.

You can find the Solution to Bettina's maze on page 95.

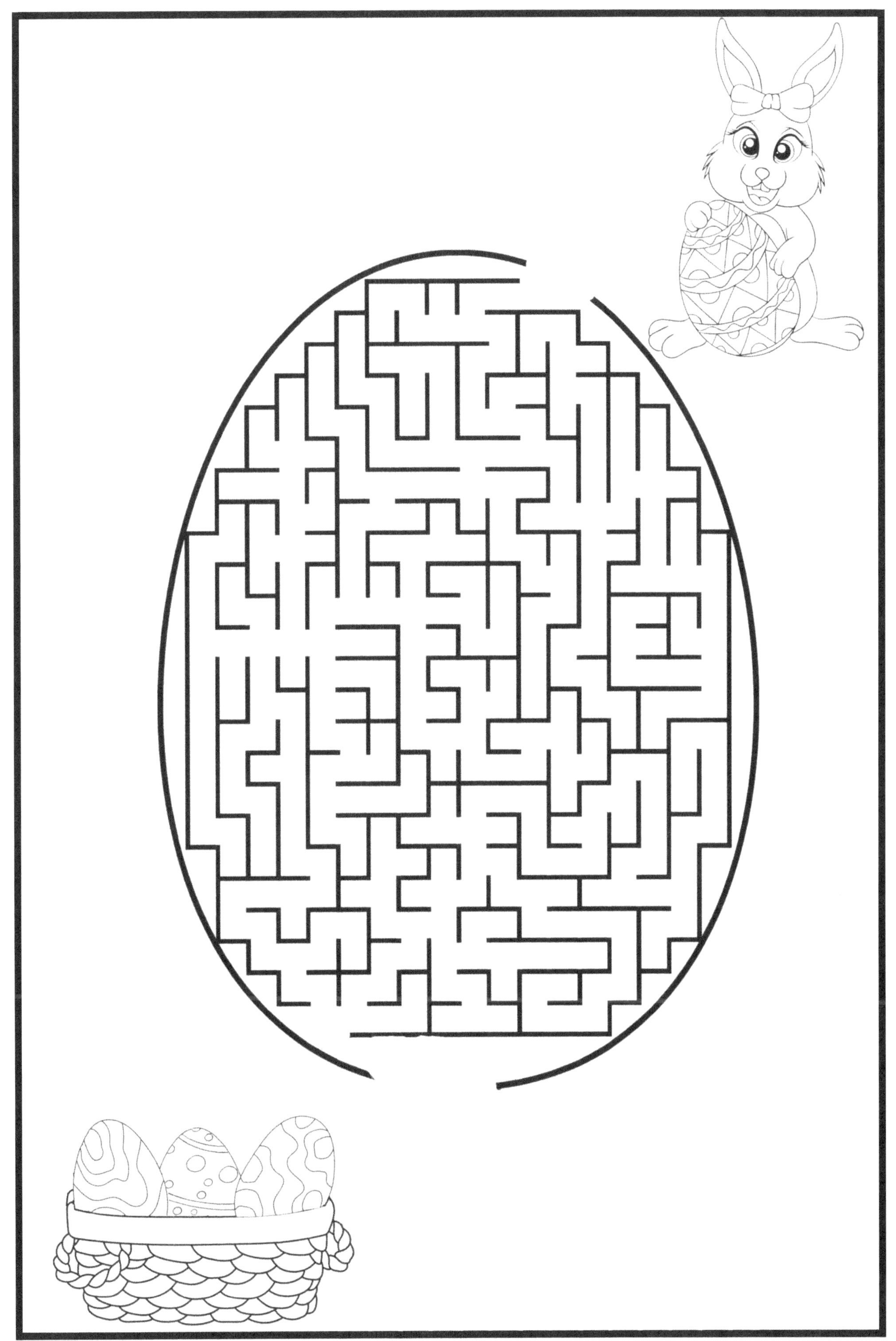

Baby **Floppie** hopes you will help him find the way to go to place his egg into the Easter basket that is getting pretty full.

You can find the Solution to Floppie's maze on page 96.

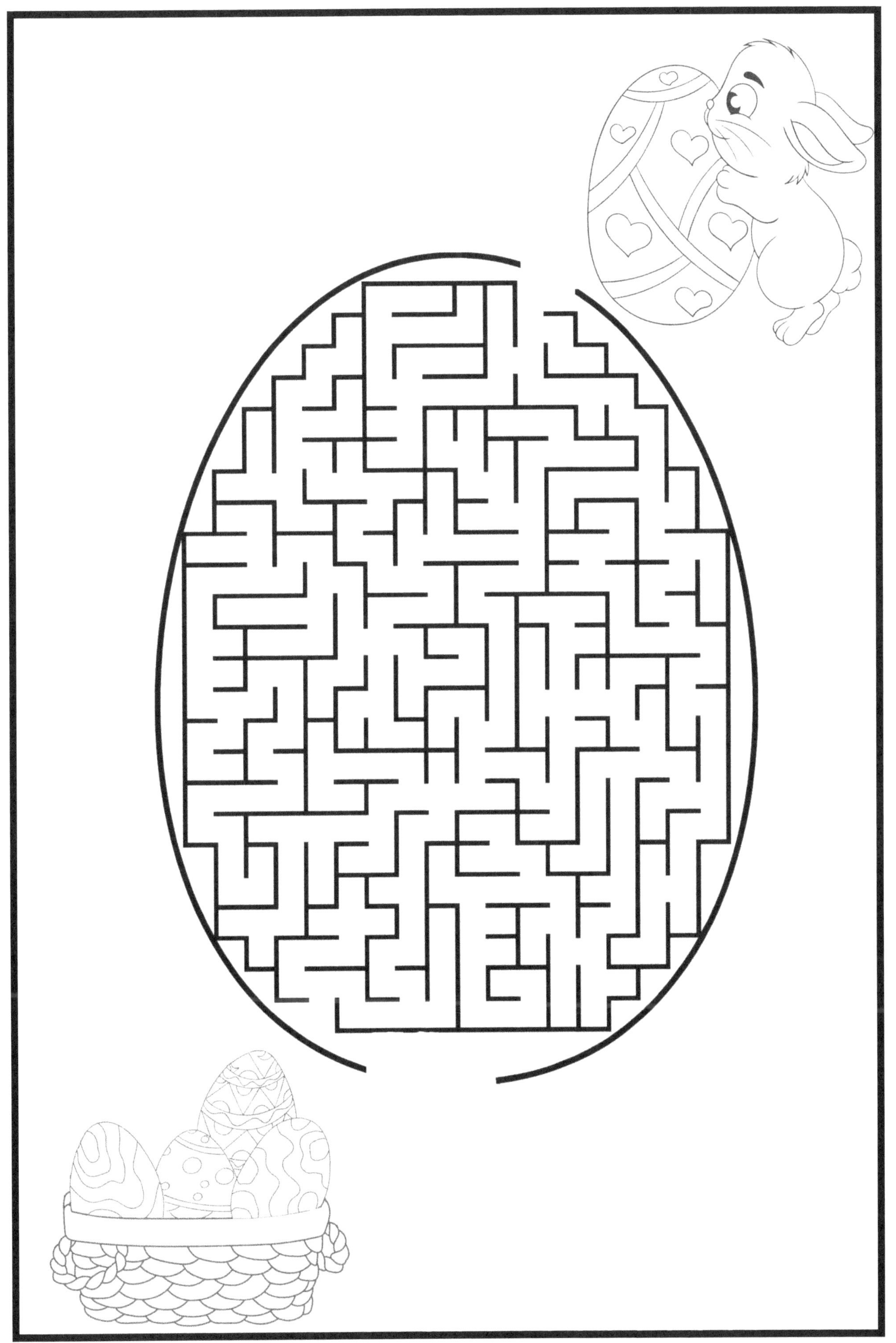

Bijou has another egg decorated with stars and needs some help from you to find the path to take to completely fill the Easter basket up with six eggs.

You can find the Solution to Bijou's maze on page 97.

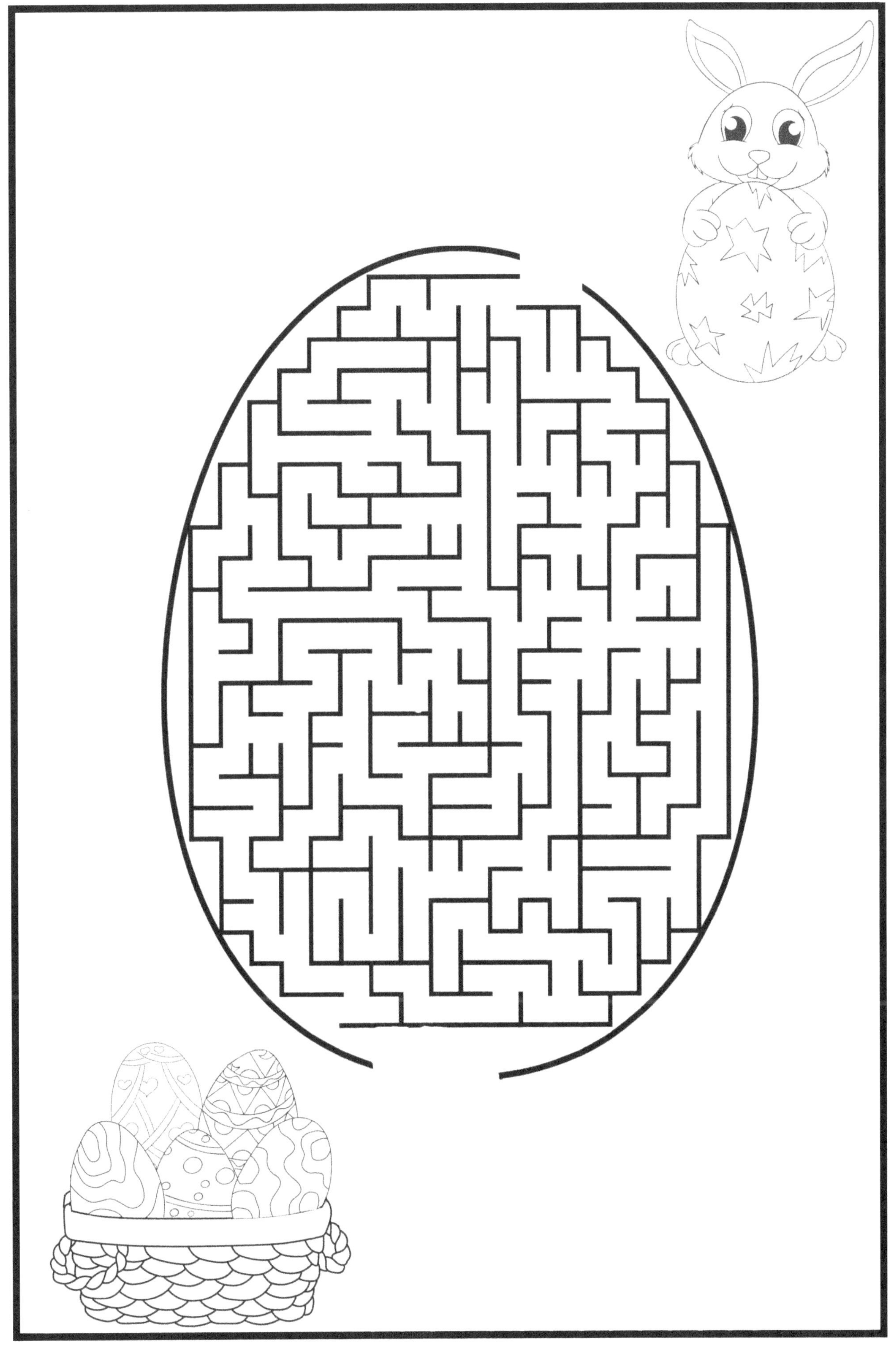

You Did it!
You helped the Joyful Heart Bunnies fill this
Easter basket with a half dozen decorated eggs
that are now waiting for you to color them.

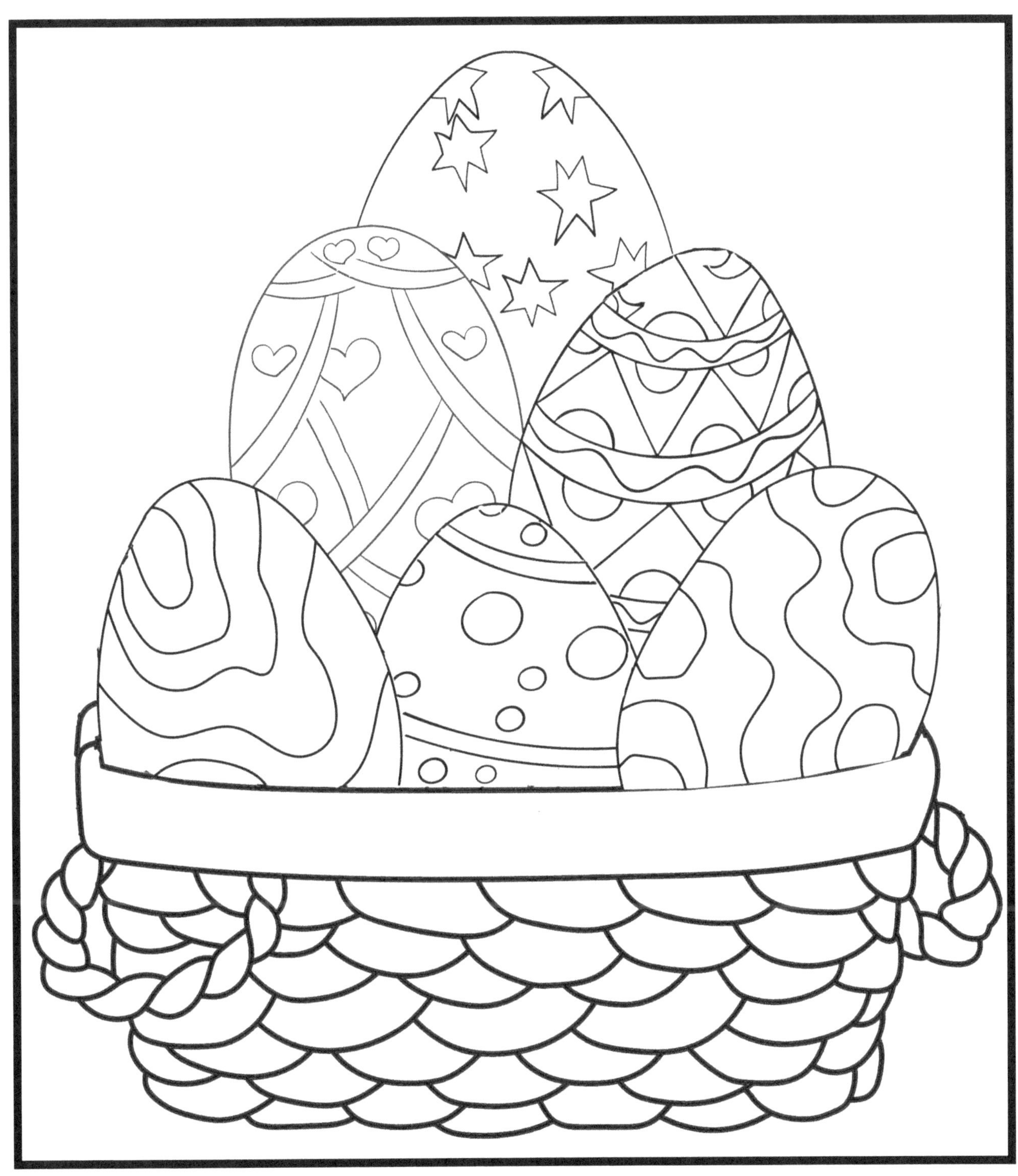

Butterflies and hearts fill the air above **DaVinci** as he enjoys decorating eggs sitting on a stump in the forest. When done, he will place them in the empty basket on another stump.

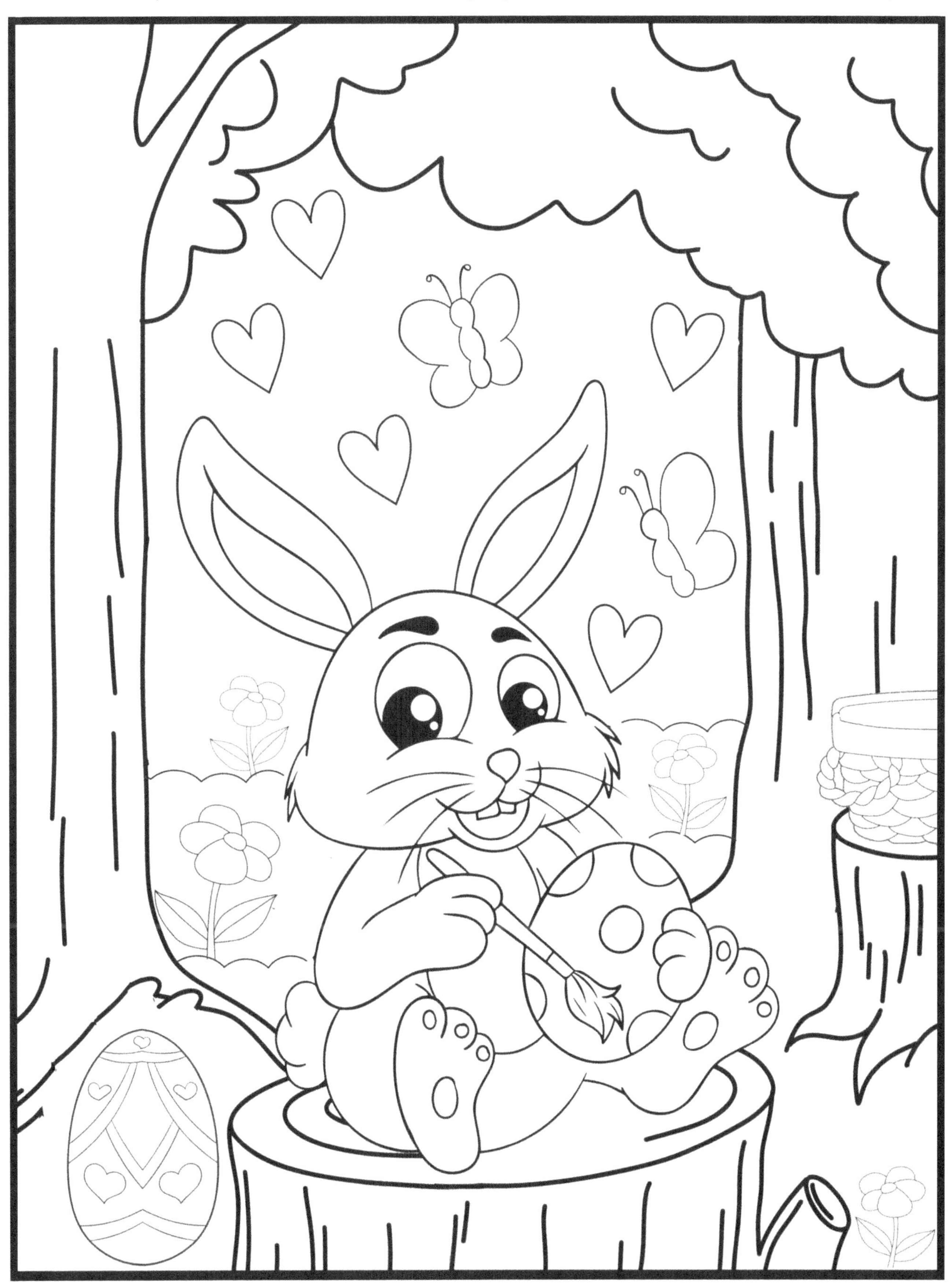

We see **Babuk** admiring a couple of decorated Easter eggs outside a window frame. Hearts fill the air and butterflies are flitting about above lovely flowers along the path.

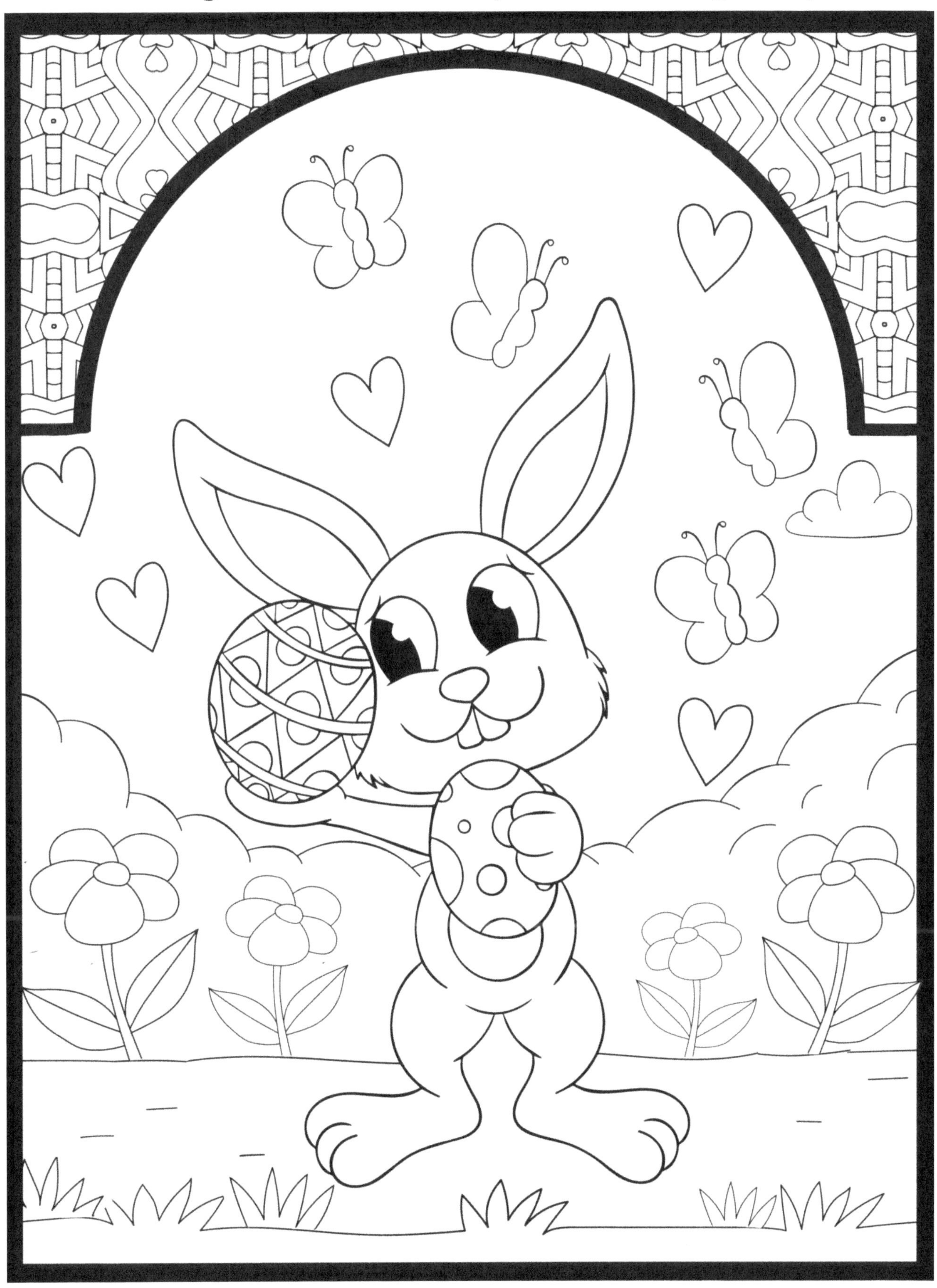

Hoppy is celebrating gathering five big decorated Easter eggs for you to color. Hearts and stars hanging on cords decorate his garden as butterflies pollinate lovely flowers.

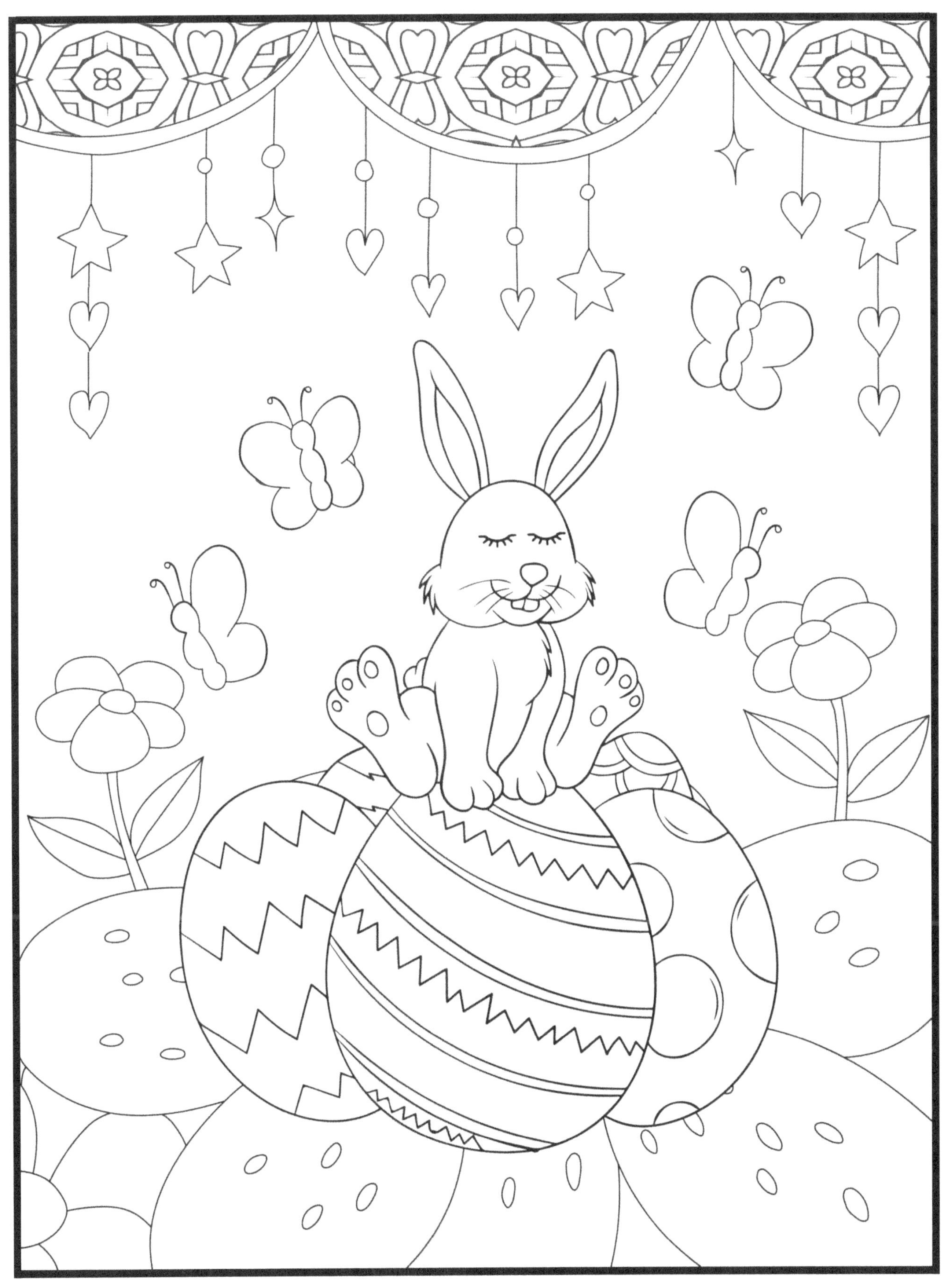

Pookie is laughing at the butterflies that are flitting from one exotic flower to another as hearts are falling from the sky on this beautiful spring day.

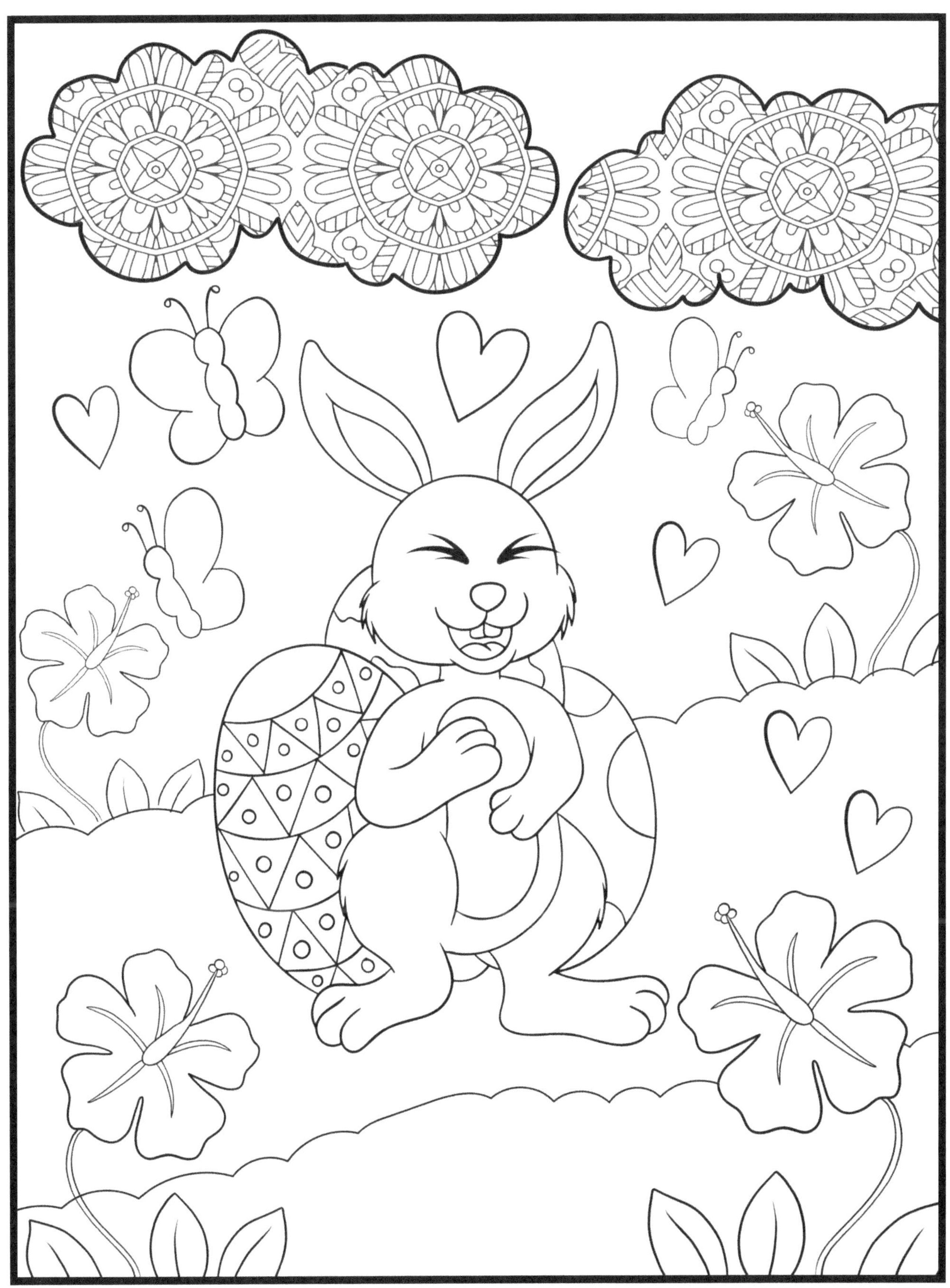

Tulips, hearts and butterflies had distracted **Pamila** from gathering up her Easter eggs. Now it's time to take them home to hide from her children to hunt and find tomorrow.

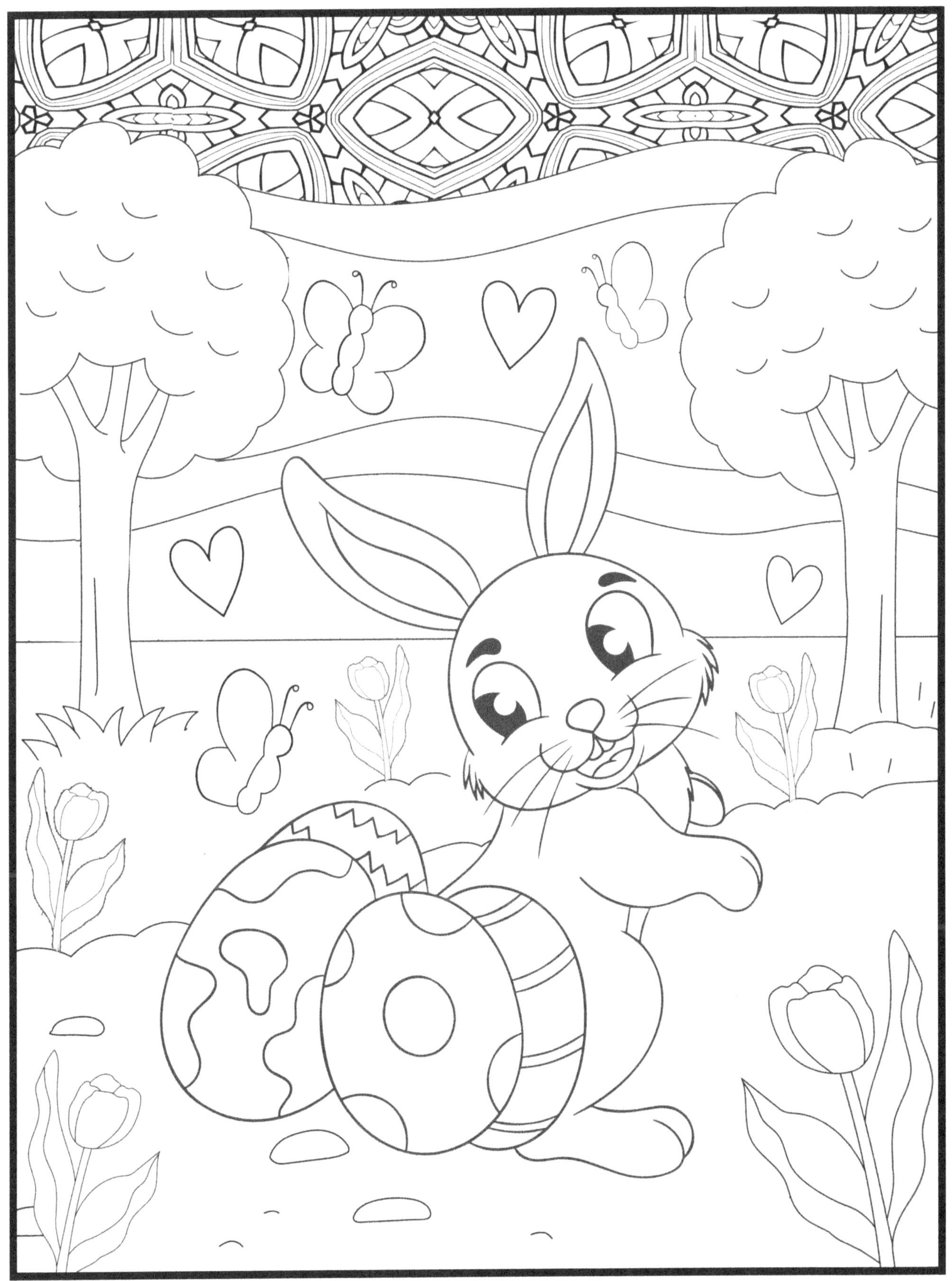

Barbriana has a heart filled with love as she holds on to her three decorated Easter eggs while watching butterflies dance under a rainbow in the sky above.

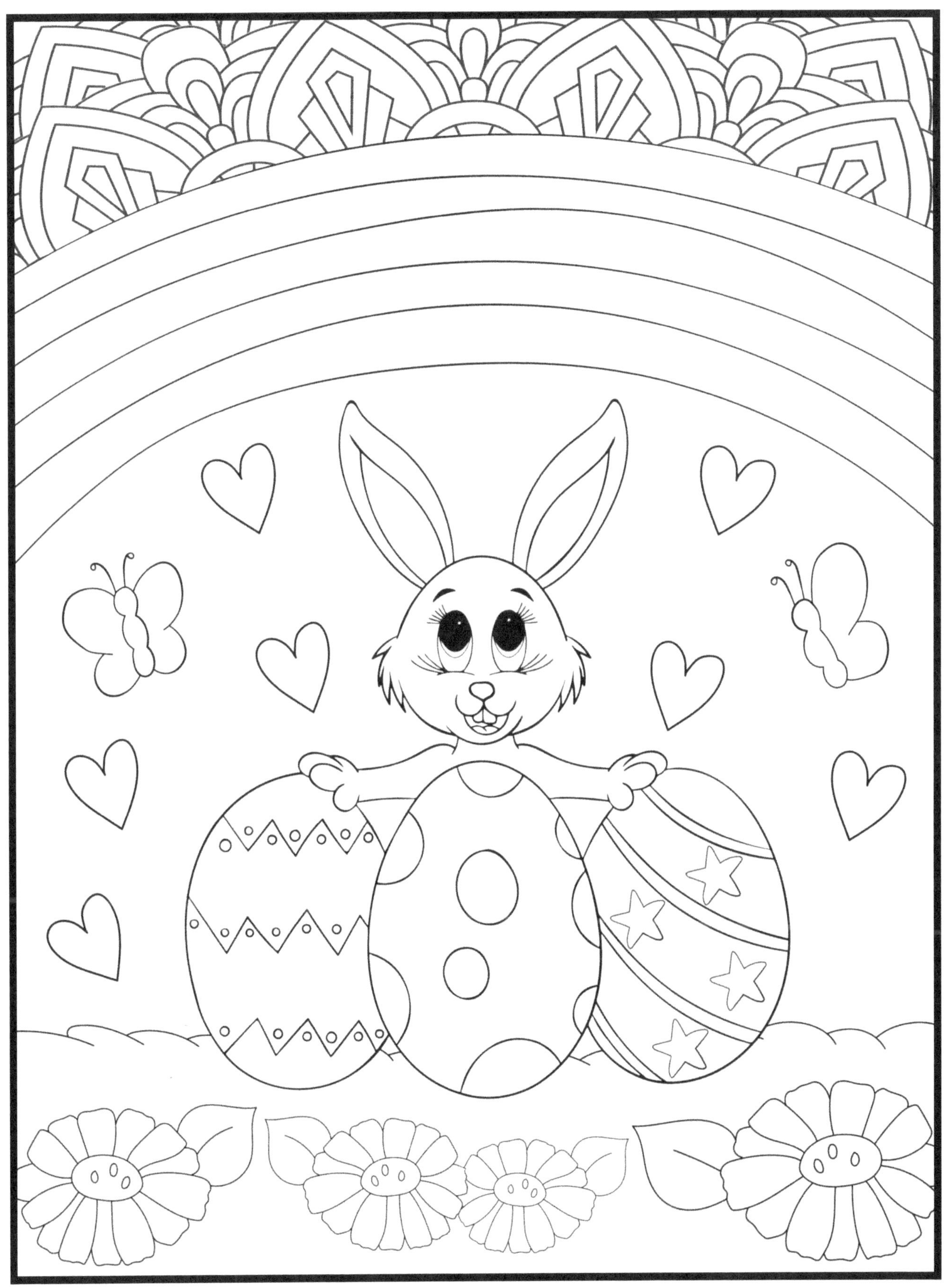

Bunny Names Word Search Puzzle.

Circle the words in the list when you find them in the square below.

Mark an X next to each word in the list when you find it.

Find the Solution on page 100.

___ BETTINA	___ BRIANNAH	___ HAREBRAIN
___ BEAUFORT	___ BLYTHE	___ SCRUFFY
___ BIGFOOTE	___ DELICATA	___ WHISKAS
___ BIJOU	___ FLOPPIE	___ YODA

I	B	I	G	F	O	O	T	E	U	W	K	F	A	E
B	J	H	D	T	S	L	A	N	I	T	T	E	B	O
F	Y	E	C	Z	B	T	K	R	F	U	P	M	E	Y
L	T	H	P	F	A	E	Y	G	H	E	D	J	A	O
A	E	T	W	C	A	O	Q	S	E	R	S	A	U	P
S	O	Y	I	F	K	D	P	U	F	L	A	H	F	C
F	A	L	D	J	C	K	O	D	J	Z	K	I	O	D
H	E	B	R	S	E	J	B	Y	S	H	S	T	R	M
D	D	T	Y	A	I	W	C	I	Y	W	I	K	T	F
F	L	S	F	B	R	I	A	N	N	A	H	F	L	V
O	Y	I	F	K	O	B	T	K	P	L	W	O	R	F
Z	J	K	U	W	L	C	E	H	Q	O	P	P	J	K
S	H	A	R	E	B	R	A	I	N	P	U	E	S	G
A	D	B	C	U	V	S	Y	K	I	F	A	D	H	T
O	L	C	S	E	P	A	R	E	B	G	Z	T	P	Y

Bunny Names and Glossary Word Search Puzzle.

Circle the words in the list when you find them in the square below.

Mark an X next to each word in the list when you find it.

Find the Solution on page 101.

___ BABUK	___ DAVINCI	___ HOPPY
___ BARBRIANA	___ DOZEN	___ MAZE
___ BASKET	___ EGGS	___ POOKIE
___ BUNNY	___ FLOWERS	___ PAMILA
___ BUTTERFLY	___ HEART	___ STARS

```
B Z Y L F R E T T U B S K F M
H E P A O S G W R B A U V U L
Y I X P B F T M Q E B O N A W
U K E Z A M L S L Y U P I N T
V A G S Z N R P O O K I E E Y
E L T P O U A B H V S M K Z L
A Y R R D A V I N C I S H O F
S M A P E S X K R B A W Y D T
I S E G I K A R Q B S Q O X U
L Z H O P P Y B P U R K R W P
R F U W E G P V L S T A R S N
Y M O S L X H Y I A G Z B M F
T X G K F L O W E R S P S I Y
W G V Q S F B Q M O E X H F L
E O L Y Q A I R F S G U R Y W
```

Things You Can Do or Color Word Search Puzzle.

Circle the words in the list when you find them in the square below.

Mark an X next to each word in the list when you find it.

Find the Solution on page 103.

___ COTTAGE	___ FLOWERS	___ MAZE	___ TULIPS
___ BUNNIES	___ FOREST	___ PATH	___ STARS
___ BASKET	___ GARDEN	___ PUZZLES	___ STUMP
___ BUTTERFLY	___ HEART	___ RAINBOW	___ SUDOKU
___ EGGS	___ HILL	___ TREE	___ WINDOW

B	K	H	U	I	R	B	U	T	T	E	R	F	L	Y
Z	E	C	S	T	O	A	U	H	P	Z	K	O	M	N
F	L	O	W	E	R	S	W	N	S	T	A	R	S	L
P	U	T	L	T	G	K	N	E	N	X	O	E	H	Y
Y	G	T	R	A	C	E	B	A	M	I	H	S	I	W
S	H	A	R	L	H	T	A	P	O	M	E	T	U	Y
C	E	G	X	A	E	P	F	E	H	A	B	S	S	Z
H	N	E	A	S	L	S	E	L	Z	Z	U	P	X	G
T	W	O	P	R	D	C	D	F	N	E	T	I	R	A
S	L	Y	W	O	D	N	I	W	C	S	M	L	K	L
M	T	B	I	K	H	E	G	U	K	O	D	U	S	D
G	R	U	A	Z	U	C	N	Y	W	U	Z	T	Y	H
I	N	O	M	D	W	O	B	N	I	A	R	X	R	I
H	E	T	D	P	M	P	L	F	G	E	B	T	I	L
F	S	U	W	N	A	S	G	G	E	H	C	O	H	L

An Egg Decorated with a Heart-based Pattern to Color.

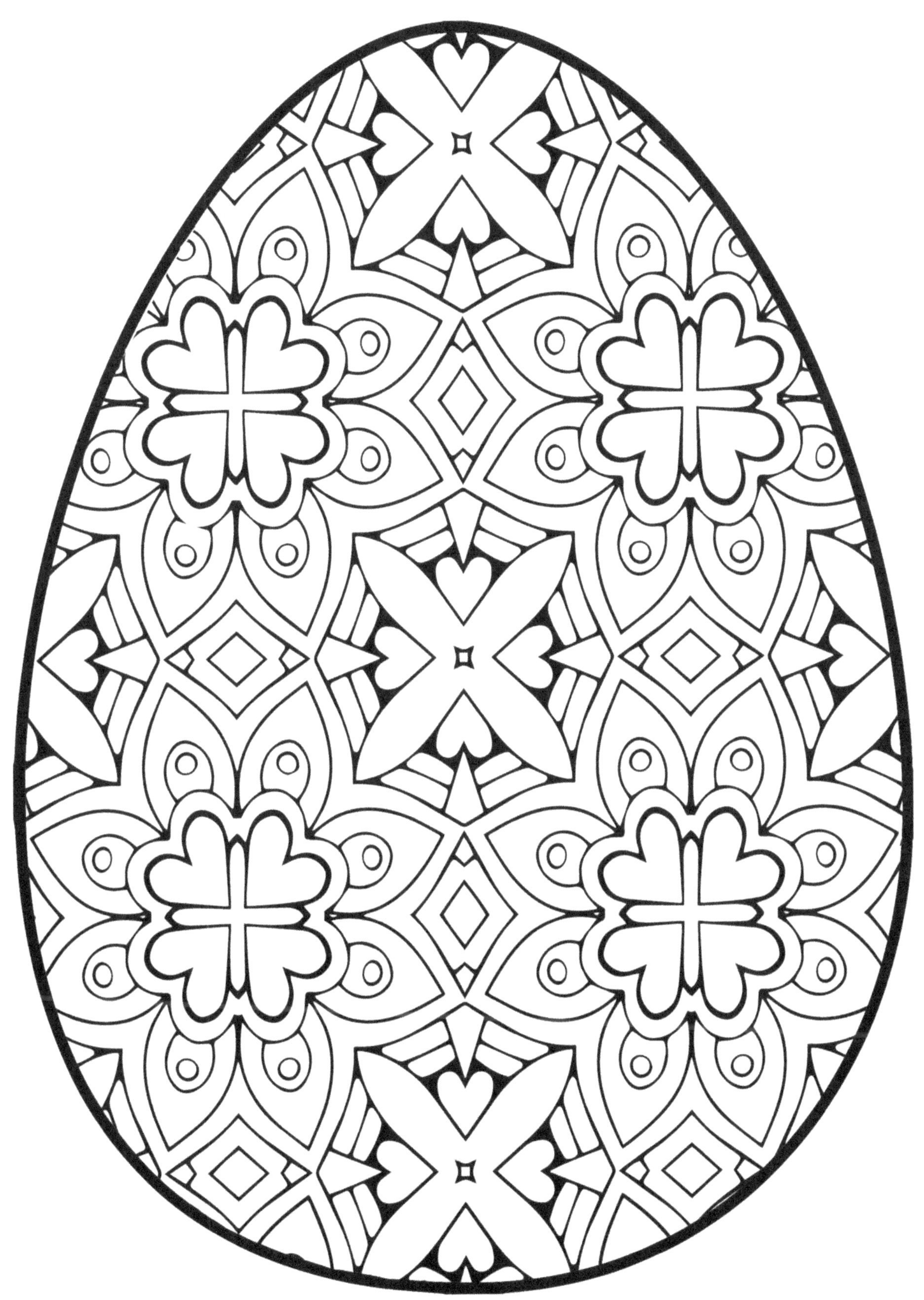

An Egg Decorated with a Heart-based Pattern to Color.

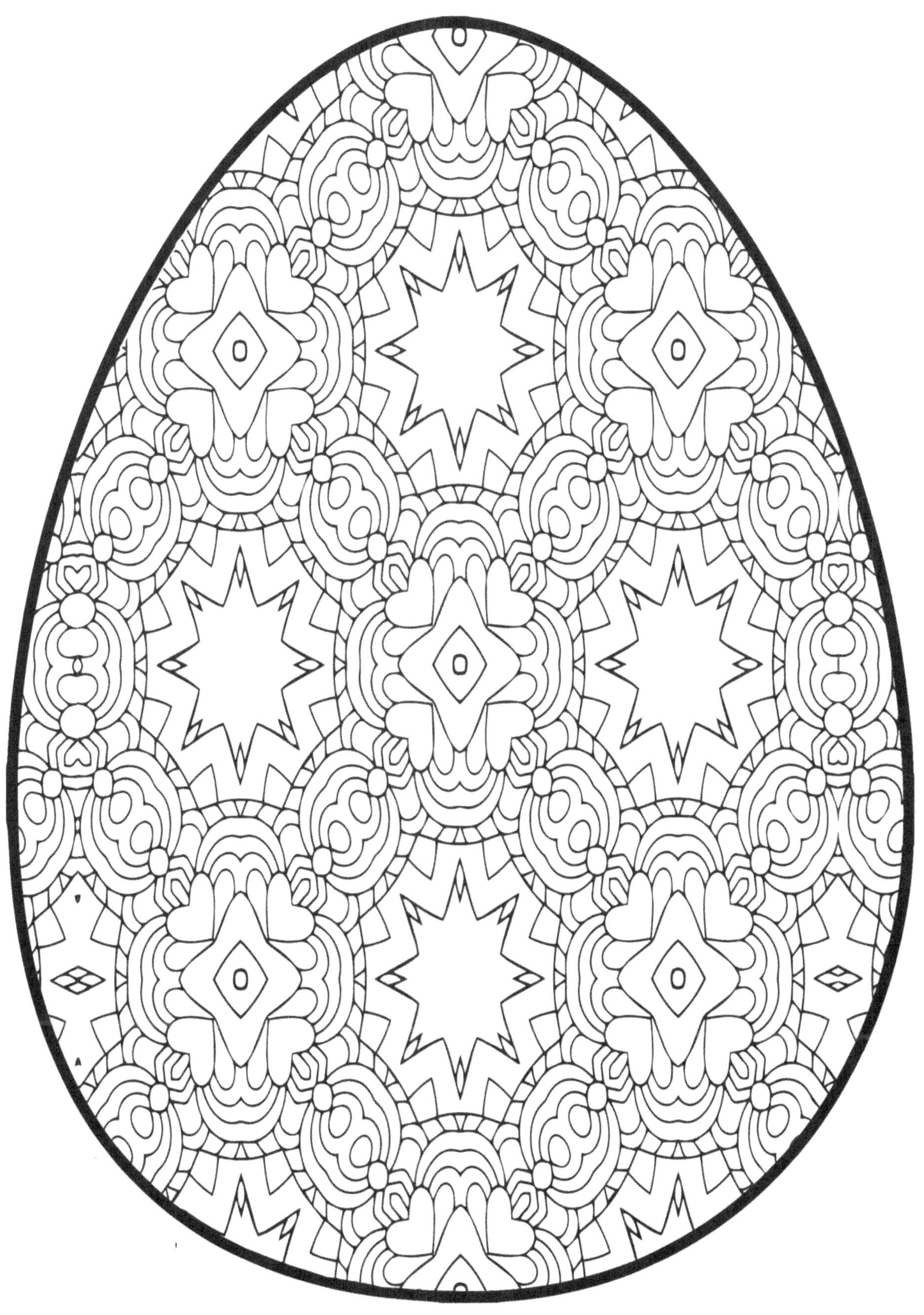

An Egg Decorated with a Heart-based Pattern to Color.

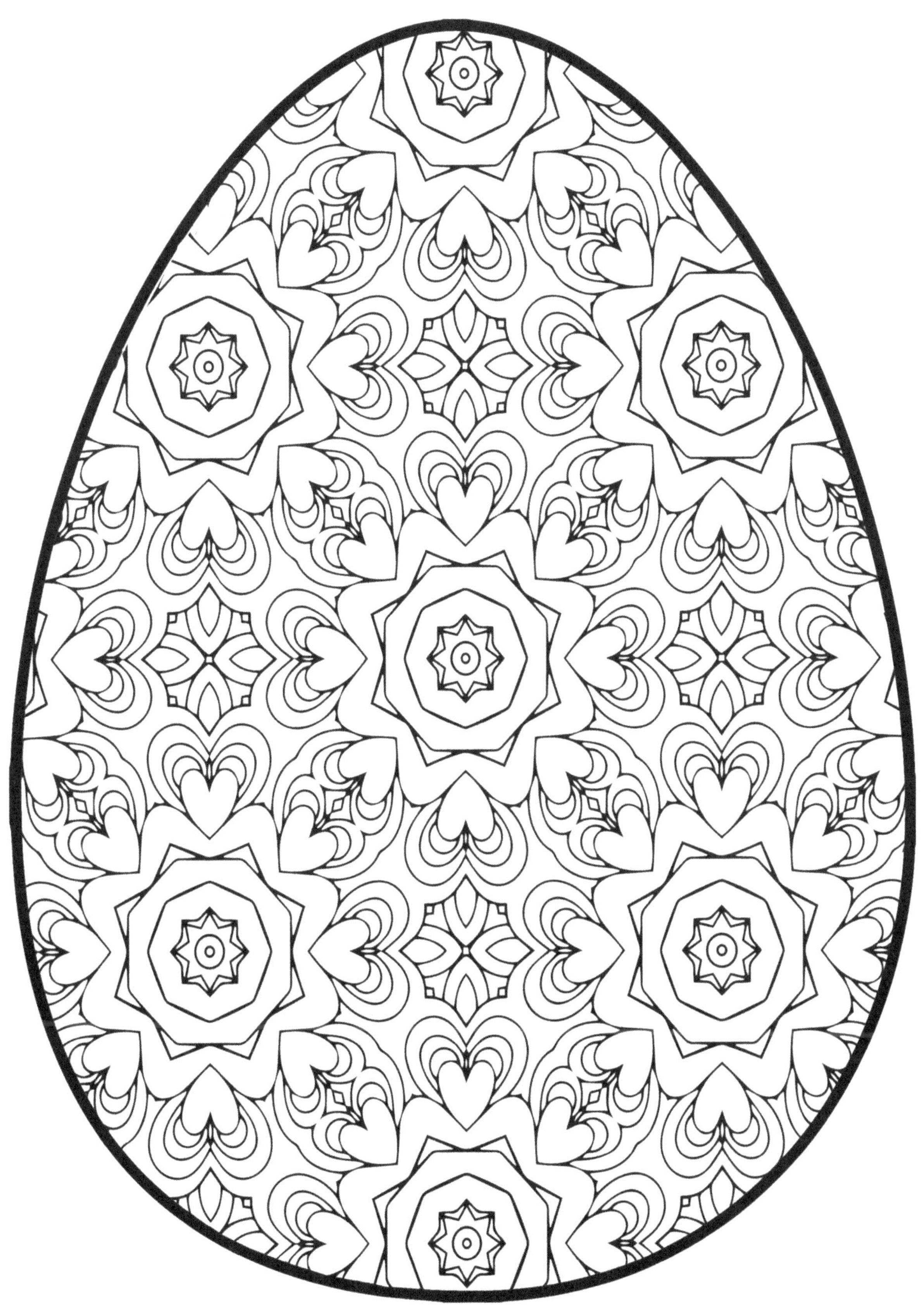

An Egg Decorated with a Heart-based Pattern to Color.

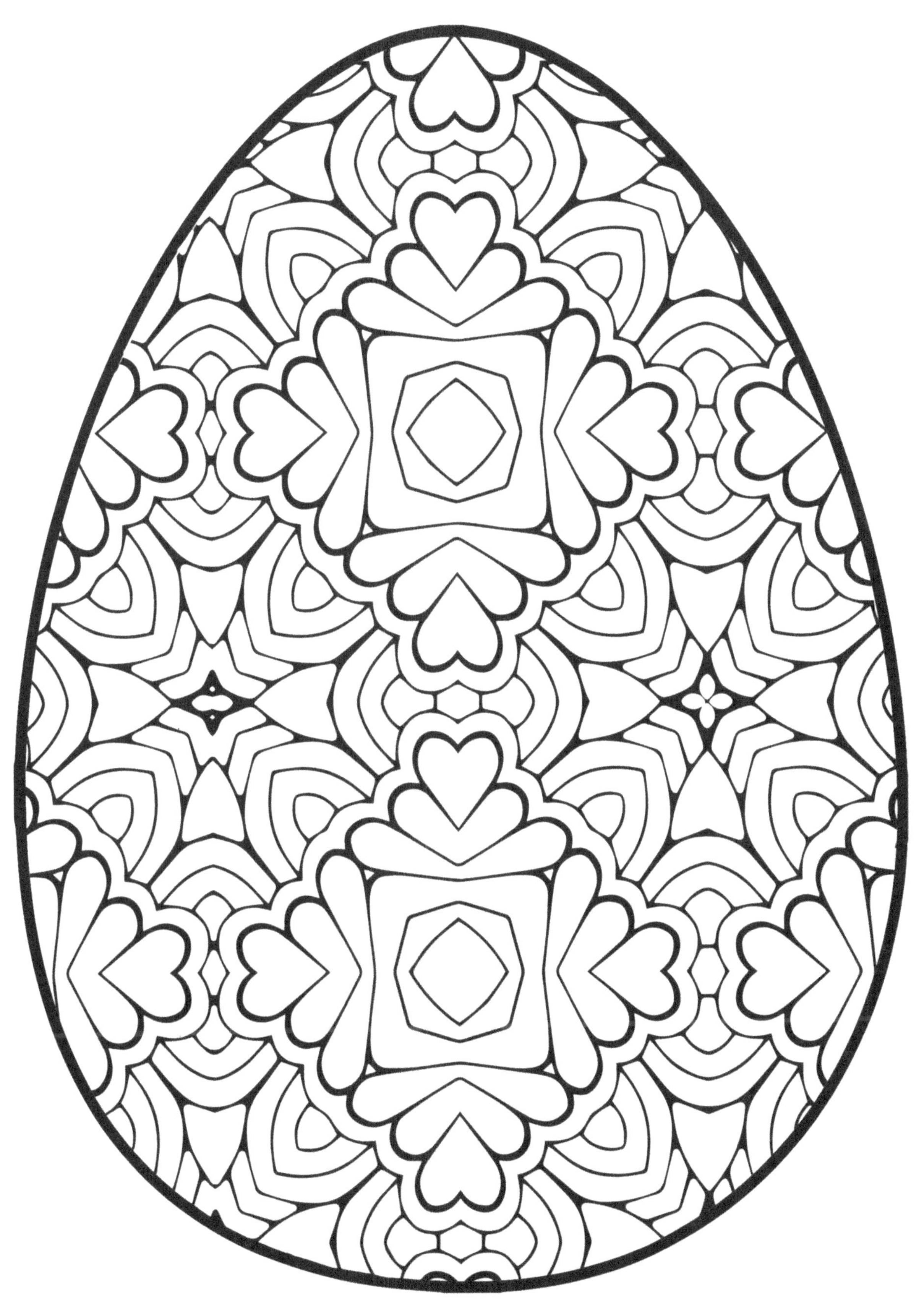

An Egg Decorated with a Heart-based Pattern to Color.

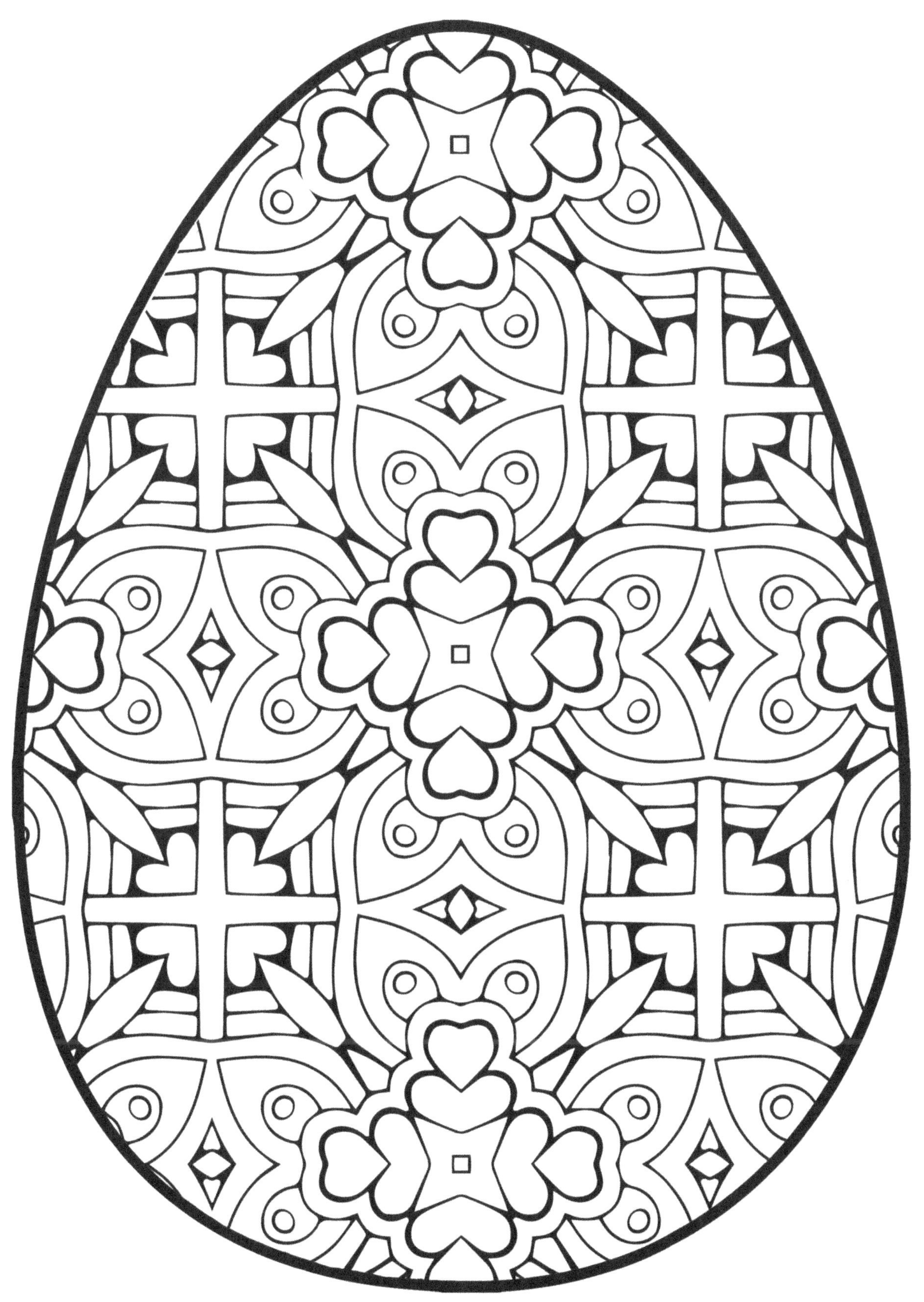

An Egg Decorated with a Heart-based Pattern to Color.

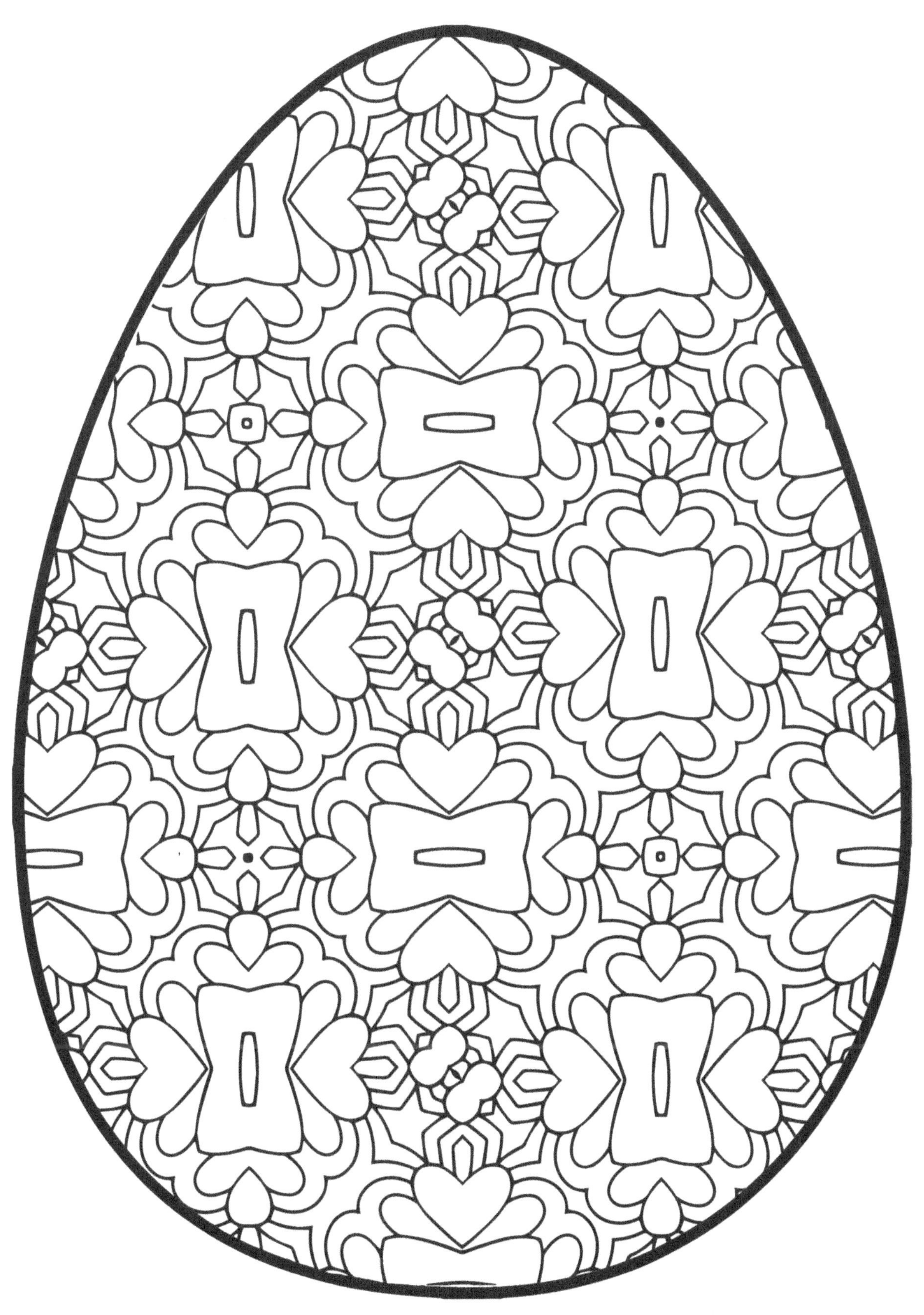

ACROSS

1. ______________ is admiring a couple of decorated Easter eggs in his hands.

2. ______________ is celebrating having gathered five big Easter eggs in his garden filled with flowers.

4. ______________ needed help to find the path to take one Easter egg to add to an empty basket.

6. ______________ is wearing a bow between her ears.

7. ______________ is painting an egg sitting on a stump in the forest.

9. ______________ is looking for more eggs among flowers and grass.

11. Beautiful tulips are making ______________ smile.

DOWN

1. Big flowers are making ______________ smile.

3. Butterflies flitting from one exotic flower to another are making ______________ laugh.

4. ______________ is standing under a rainbow.

5. ______________ wants to add an Easter egg decorated with hearts into a basket at the bottom of a maze.

6. Hearts are dancing in the sky above ______________.

7. ______________ is holding an Easter egg with circles and stripes to carry to the basket at the bottom of a maze.

8. ______________ was distracted by tulips, floating hearts and butterflies

10. ______________ has an Easter egg decorated with stars to fill up a basket at the bottom of a maze.

Bunny Name Crossword Puzzle.

Find the Solution on page 105.

Clues for the Bunny Glossary Words Crossword Puzzle.

ACROSS

1. Barbriana is standing under a _____________.
4. DaVinci is sitting on a _____________.
5. _____________ stars and hearts fill the air above Harebrain.
7. The Bunnies Easter baskets are filled with decorated _____________.
9. Harebrain wants to get home to _____________ some Easter eggs for his children.
13. _____________ are in the field that Whiskas will walk past on a path going up a hill.
15. Lovely _____________ are blooming in Hoppy's garden.
16. Whiskas is headed to a neighbor's _____________ with her Easter basket filled with decorated eggs.
17. There is a _____________ filled with six Easter eggs for you to color on page 31.
18. All the bunnies have _____________ Easter eggs.

DOWN

2. _____________ are distracting Pamila from gathering up four patterned Easter eggs.
3. Butterflies are _____________ around Babuk.
6. Hoppy has decorated his _____________ with stars and hearts hanging down on cords.
8. The sky above Blythe is filled with _____________ and hearts.
9. _____________ are joyfully dancing in the sky to welcome Briannah home.
10. Butterflies fly from flower to flower to _____________ them.
11. We can see Babuk holding two Easter eggs through a _____________.
12. Hoppy took some time to _____________ having four large Easter eggs in his garden.
14. Barbriana has her heart filled with _____________.

Bunny Glossary Words Crossword Puzzle.

Find the Solution on page 107.

An Easter Egg with a Flowery Design to Color.

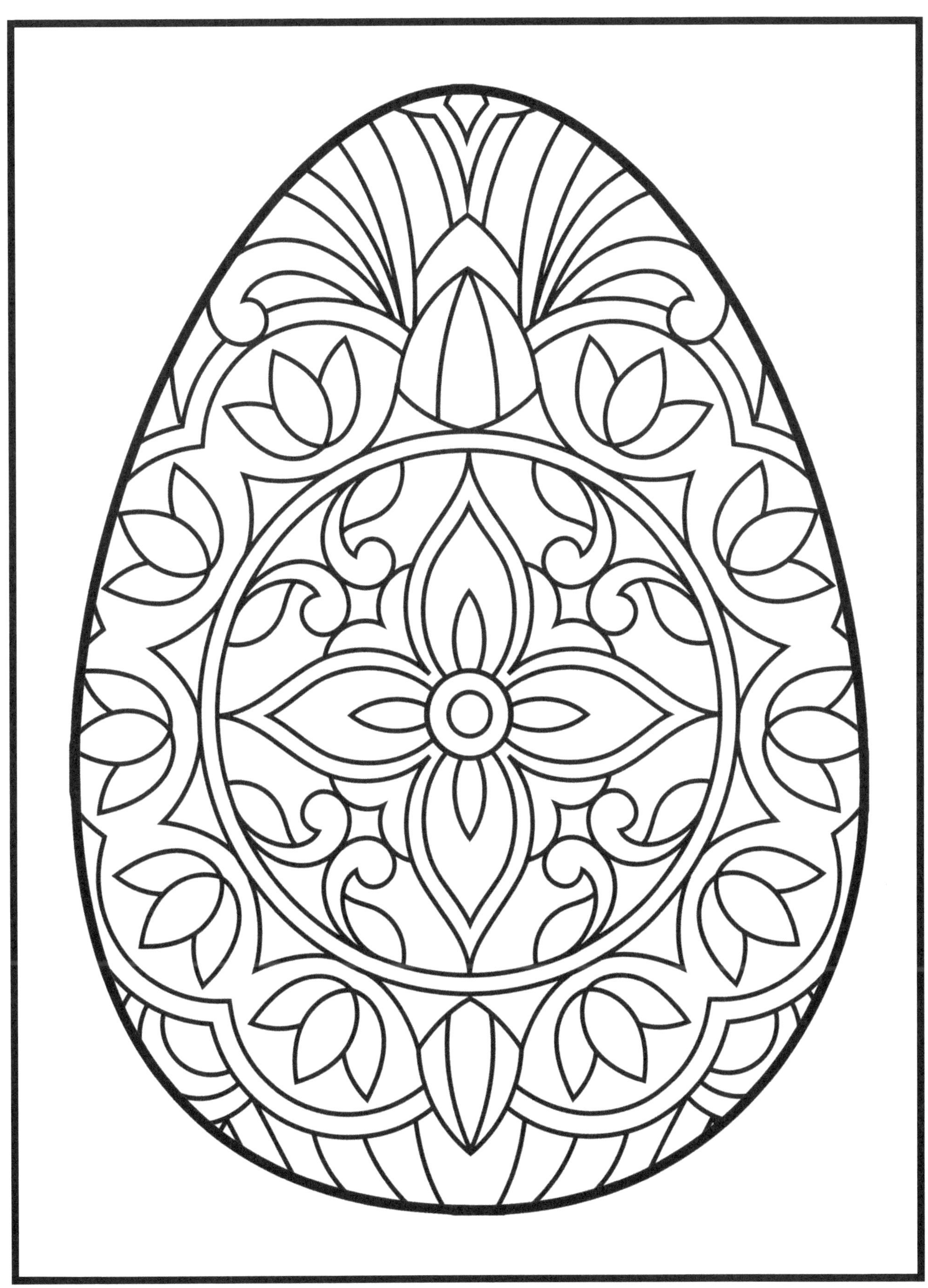

An Easter Egg with a Flowery Design to Color.

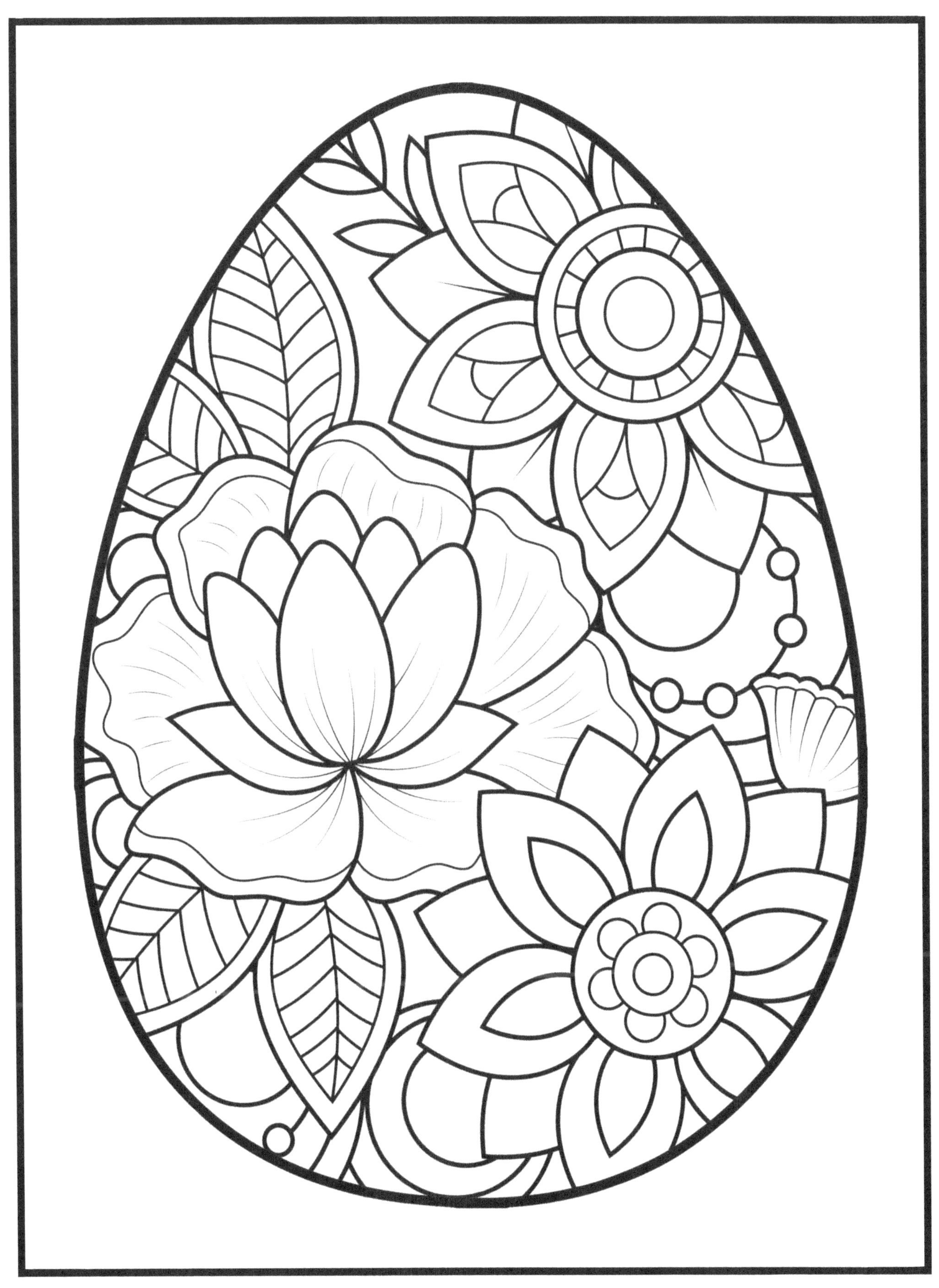

An Easter Egg with a Flowery Design to Color.

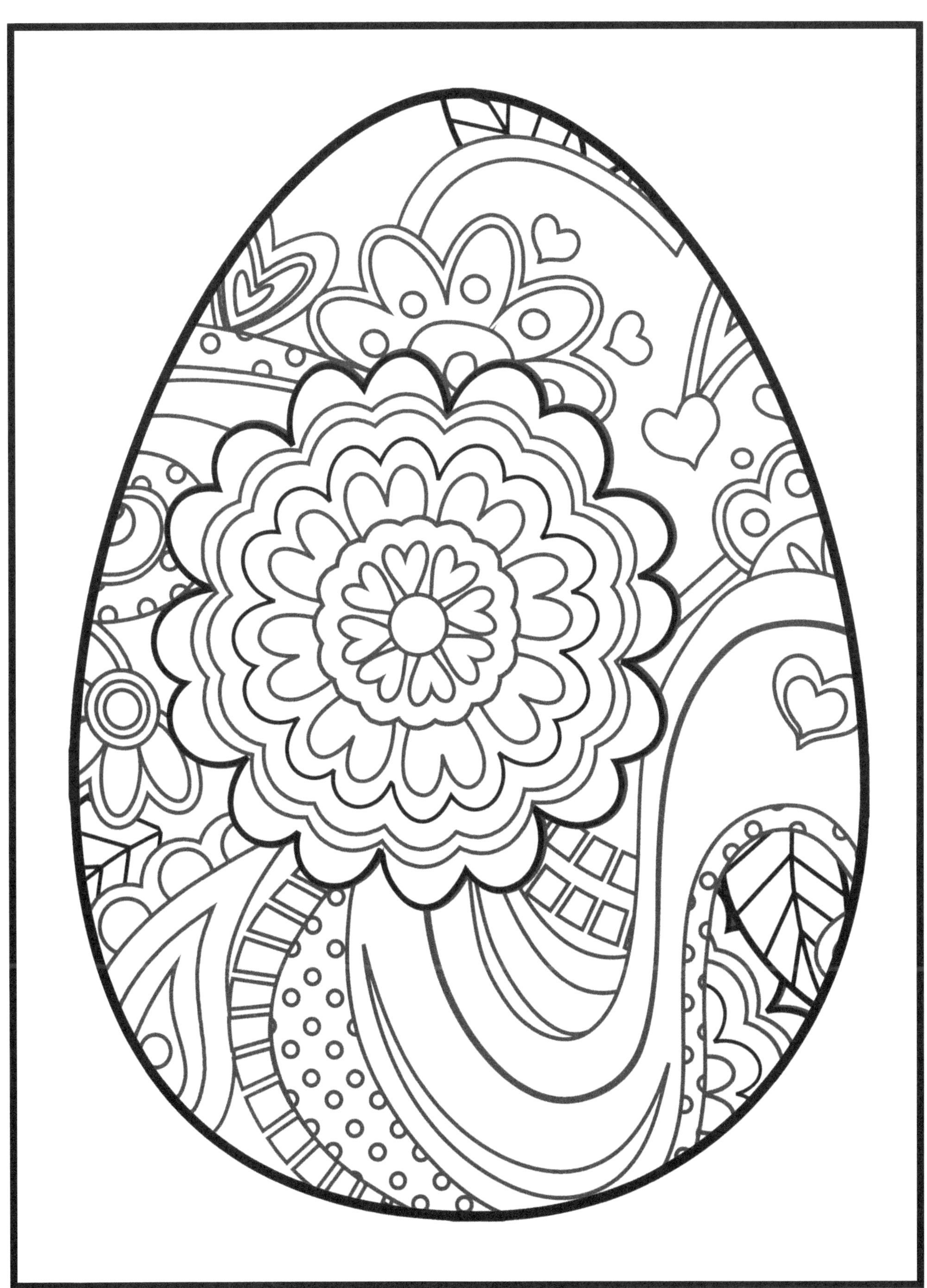

An Easter Egg with a Flowery Design to Color.

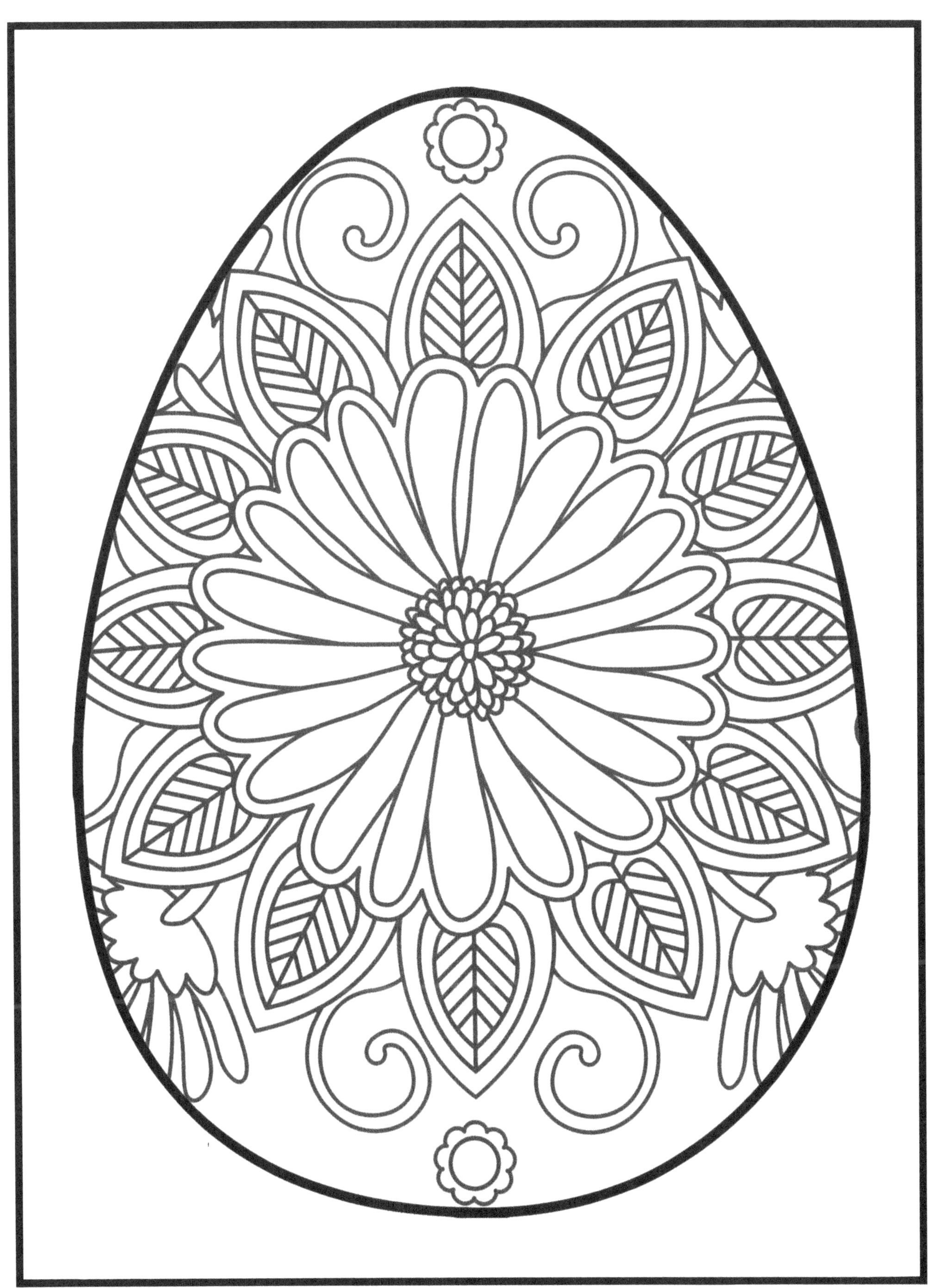

An Easter Egg with a Flowery Design to Color.

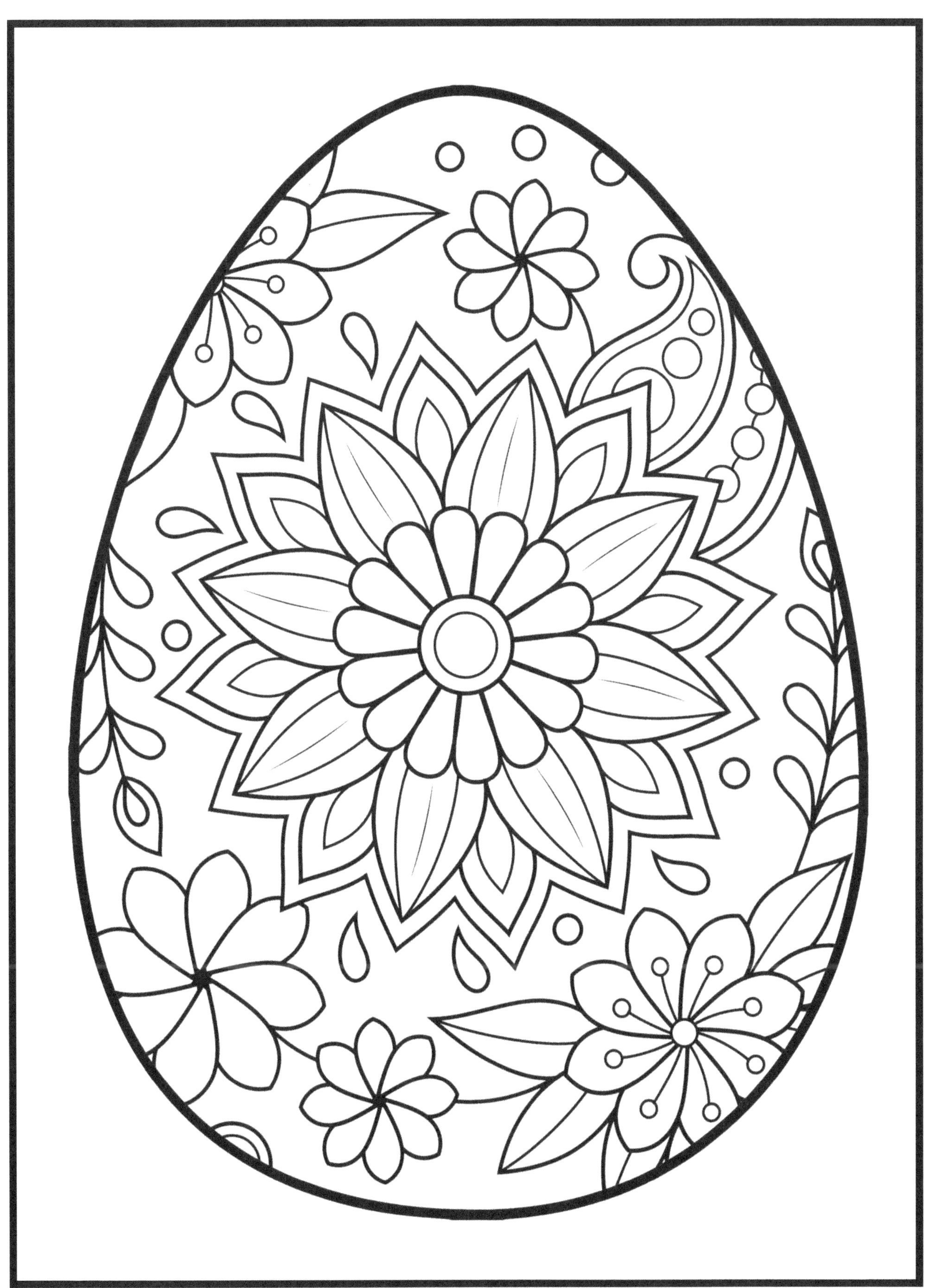

An Easter Egg with a Flowery Design to Color.

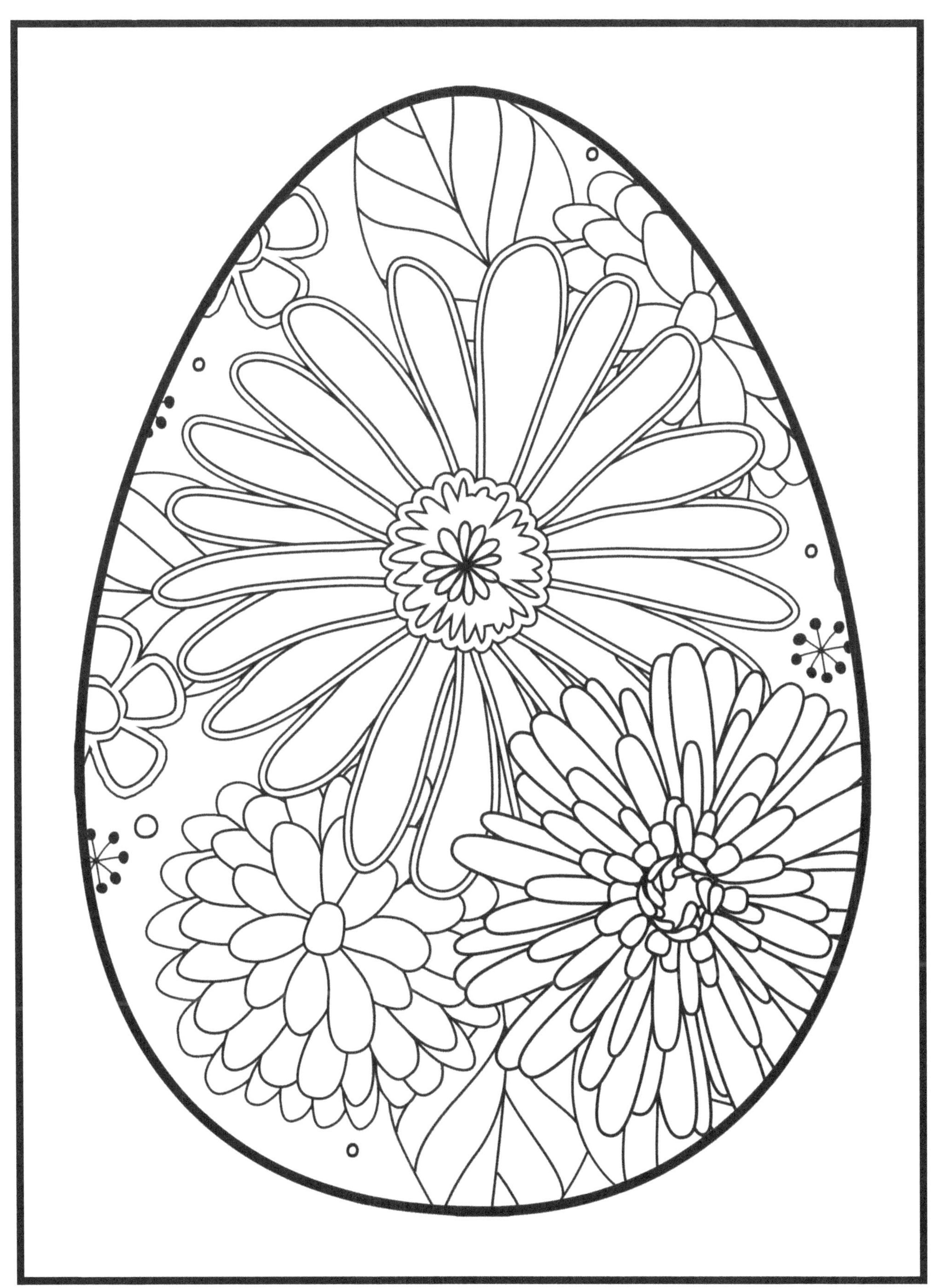

Eggs, Hearts, Flowers and Stars Sudoku #1

This Sudoku Puzzle has a unique solution that can be reached in a logical manner.
Draw one of the four images into each of the blank spaces so that each row and column in the 4x4 box contains an egg, a heart, a flower and a star without repeating that image in the row or column.

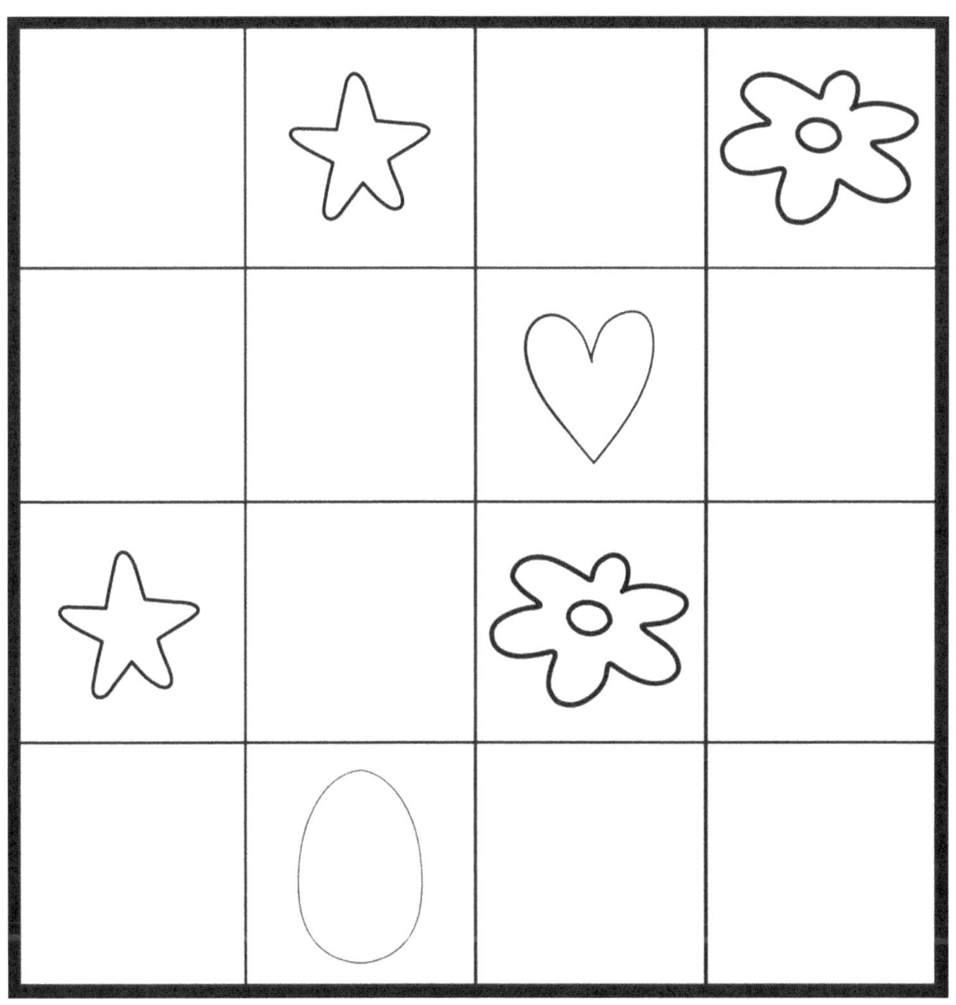

You can find the Solution to Sudoku #1 on page 108.

Eggs, Hearts, Flowers and Stars Sudoku #2

This Sudoku Puzzle has a unique solution that can be reached in a logical manner.
Draw one of the four images into each of the blank spaces so that each row and column in the 4x4 box contains an egg, a heart, a flower and a star without repeating that image in the row or column.

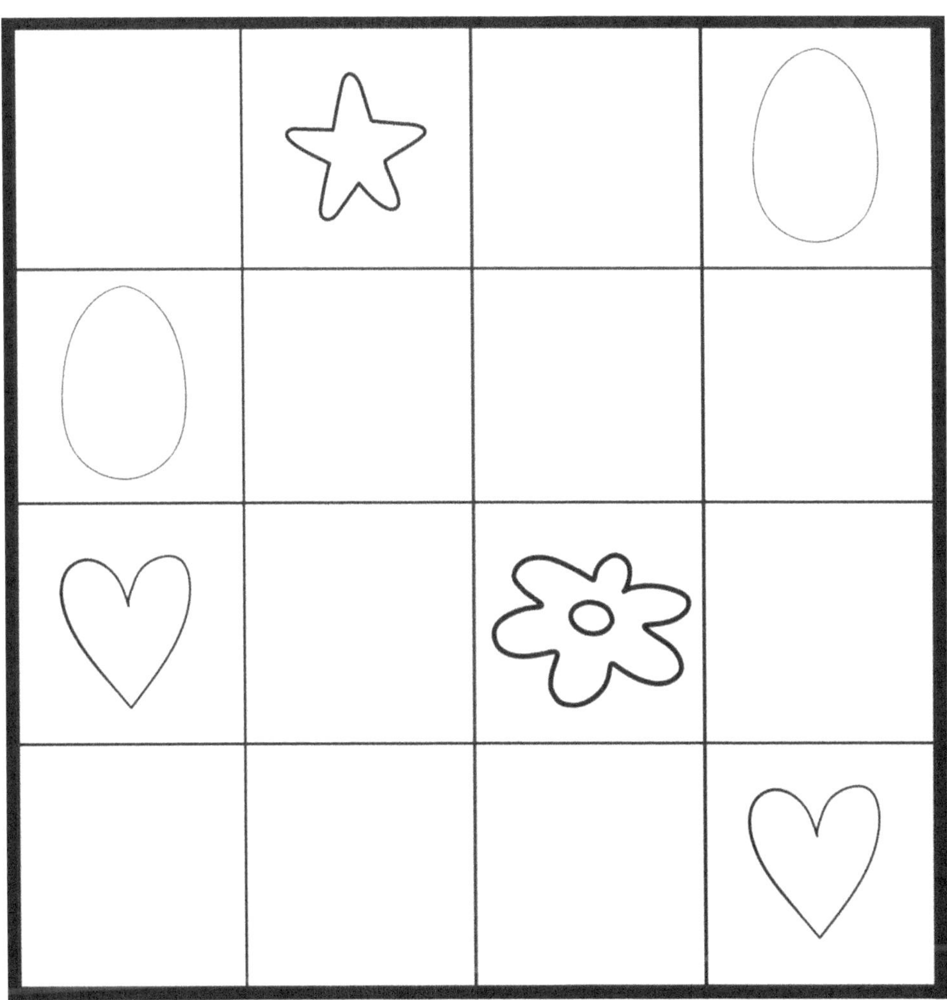

You can find the Solution to Sudoku #2 on page 109.

Eggs, Hearts, Flowers and Stars Sudoku #3

This Sudoku Puzzle has a unique solution that can be reached in a logical manner.
Draw one of the four images into each of the blank spaces so that each row and column in the 4x4 box contains an egg, a heart, a flower and a star without repeating that image in the row or column.

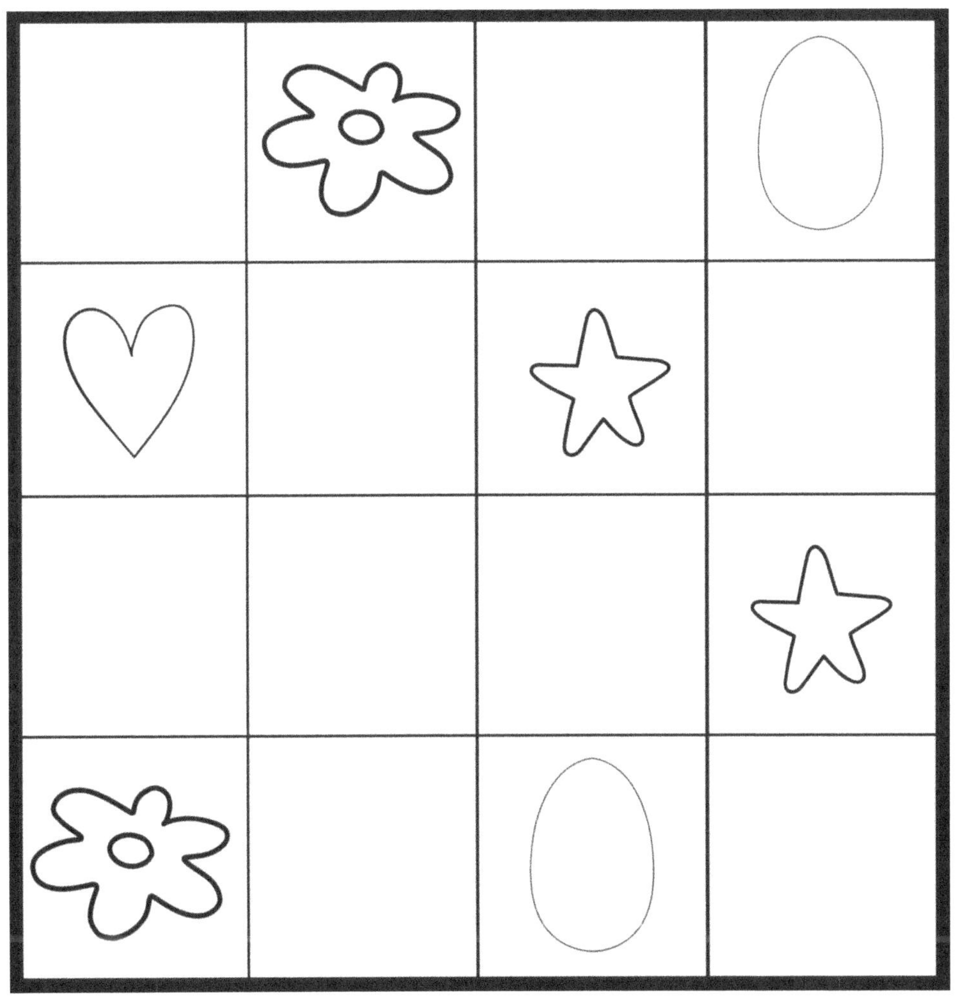

You can find the Solution to Sudoku #3 on page 110.

Eggs, Hearts, Flowers and Stars Sudoku #4

This Sudoku Puzzle has a unique solution that can be reached in a logical manner.
Draw one of the four images into each of the blank spaces so that each row and column in the 4x4 box contains an egg, a heart, a flower and a star without repeating that image in the row or column.

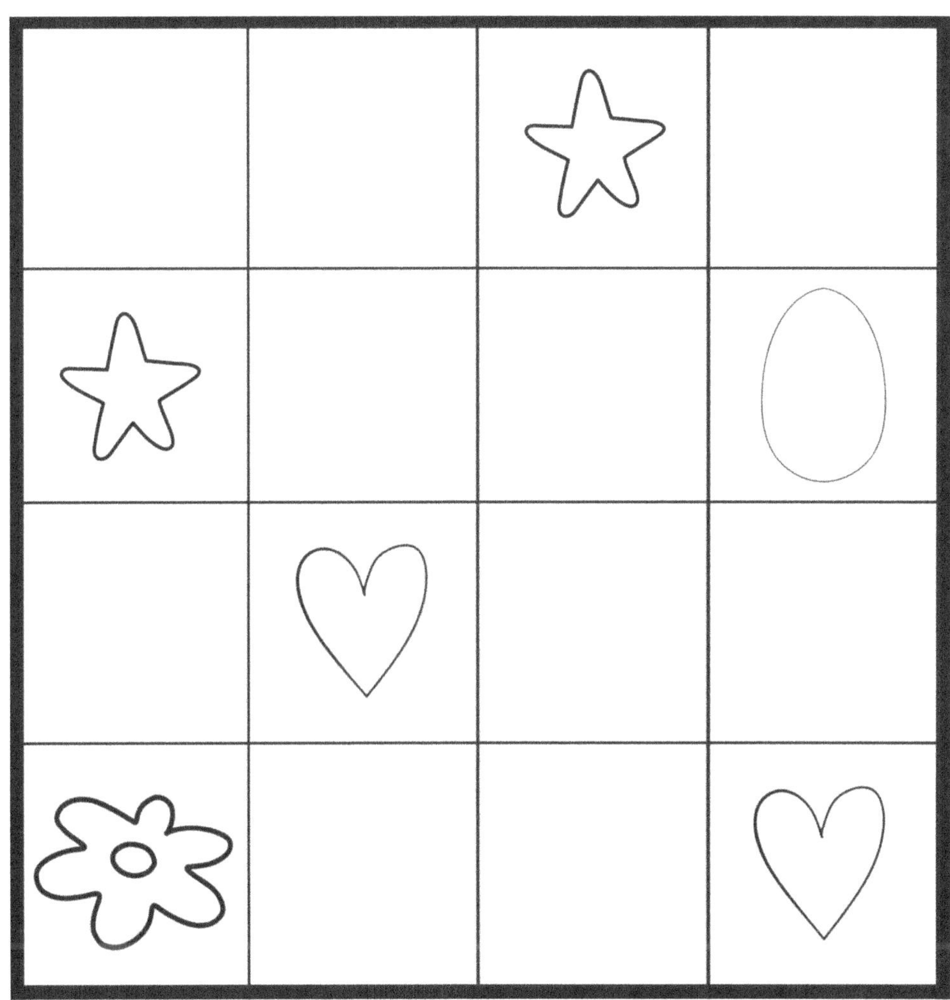

You can find the Solution to Sudoku #4 on page 111.

Eggs, Hearts, Flowers and Stars Sudoku #5

This Sudoku Puzzle has a unique solution that can be reached in a logical manner.
Draw one of the four images into each of the blank spaces so that each row and column in the 4x4 box contains an egg, a heart, a flower and a star without repeating that image in the row or column.

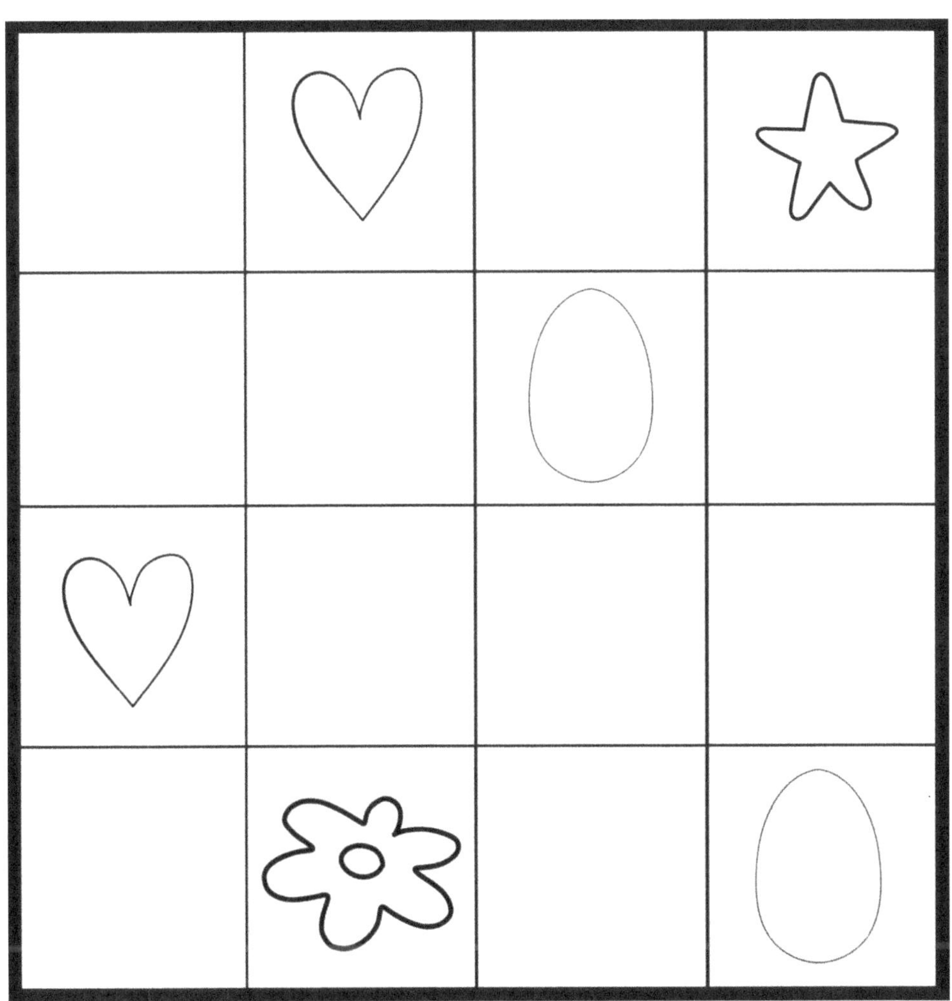

You can find the Solution to Sudoku #5 on page 112.

Eggs, Hearts, Flowers and Stars Sudoku #6

This Sudoku Puzzle has a unique solution that can be reached in a logical manner.
Draw one of the four images into each of the blank spaces so that each row and column in the 4x4 box contains an egg, a heart, a flower and a star without repeating that image in the row or column.

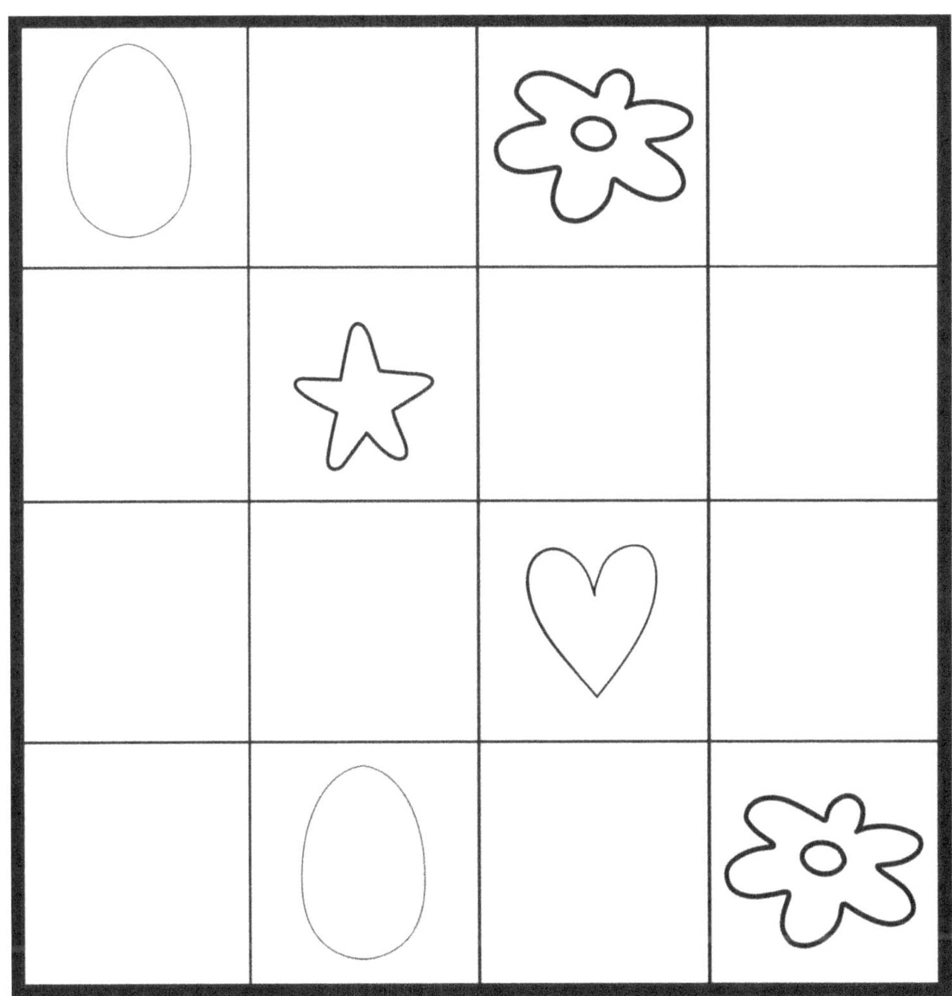

You can find the Solution to Sudoku #6 on page 113.

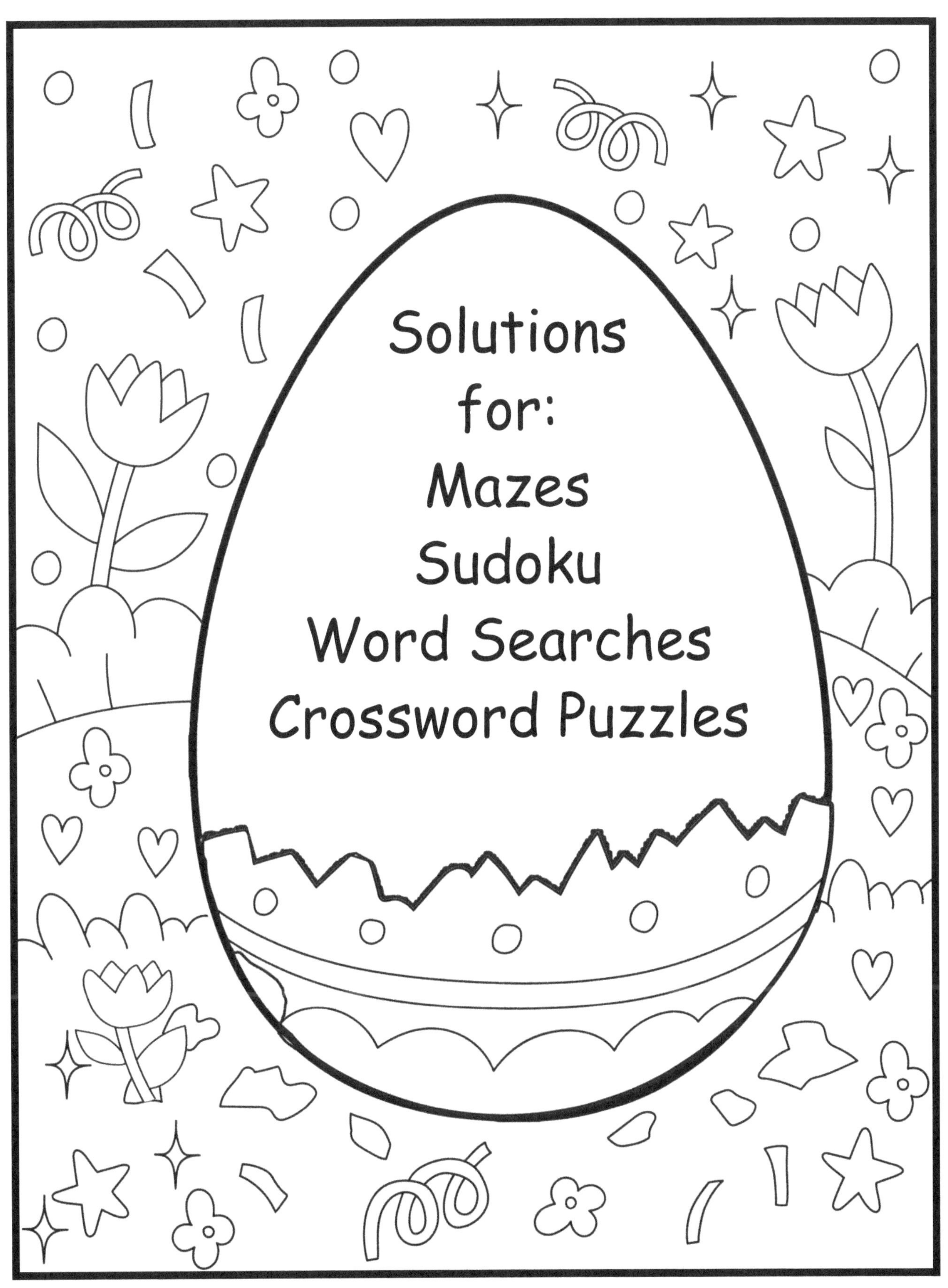

Solutions
for:
Mazes
Sudoku
Word Searches
Crossword Puzzles

Solution for Bigfoote's
Maze on page 19.

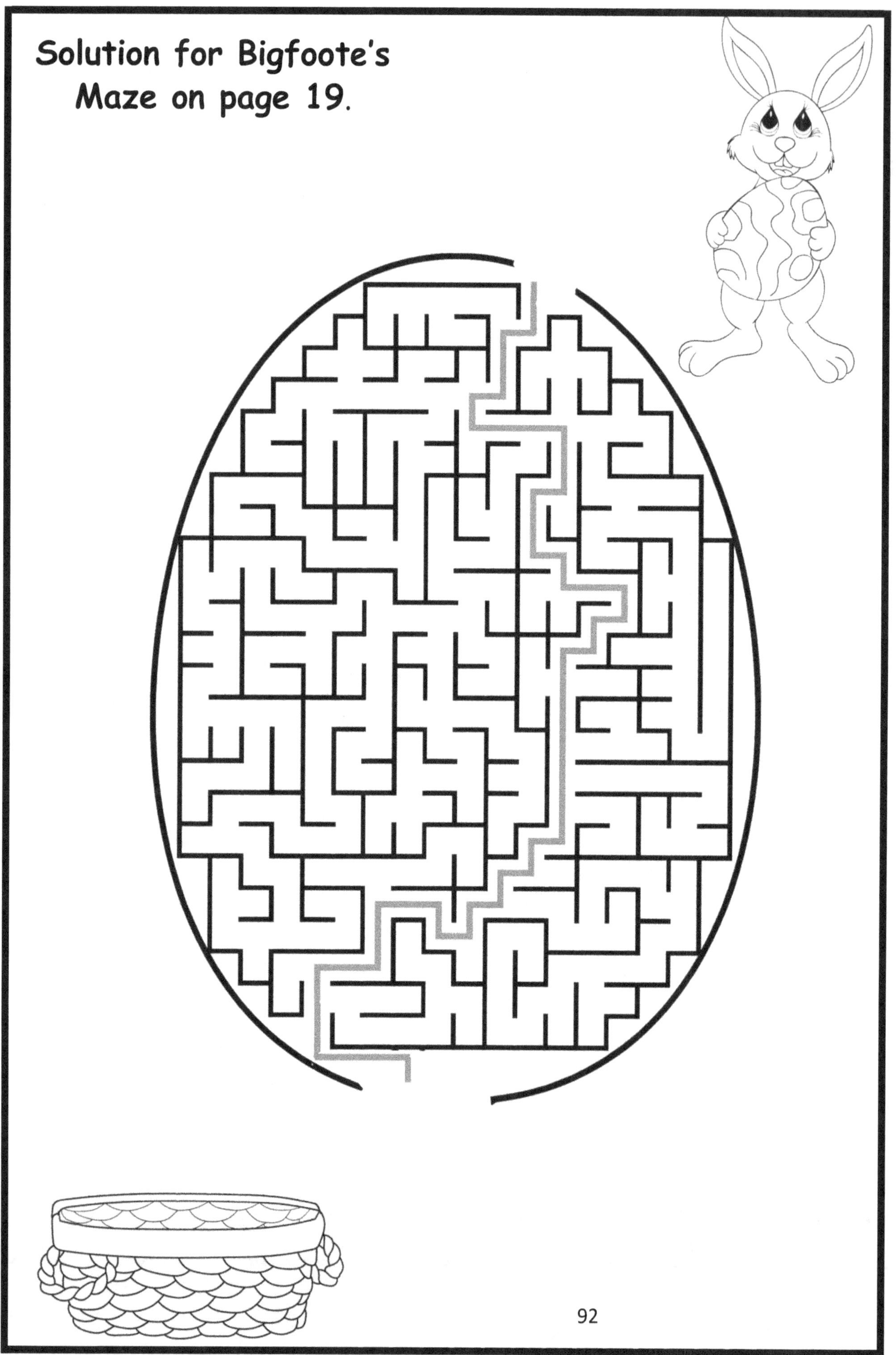

Solution for Yoda's
Maze on page 21.

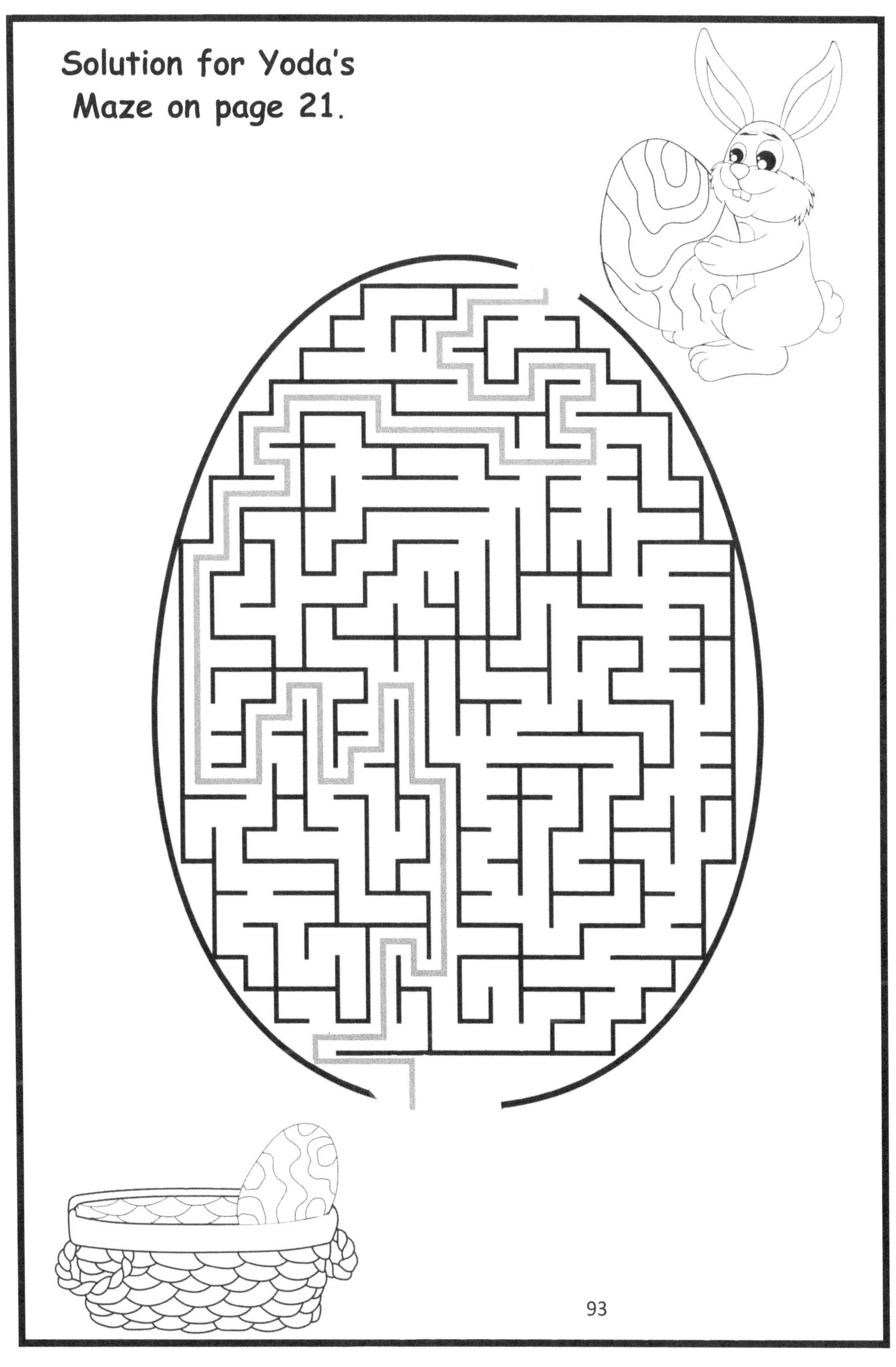

Solution for Delicata's Maze on page 23.

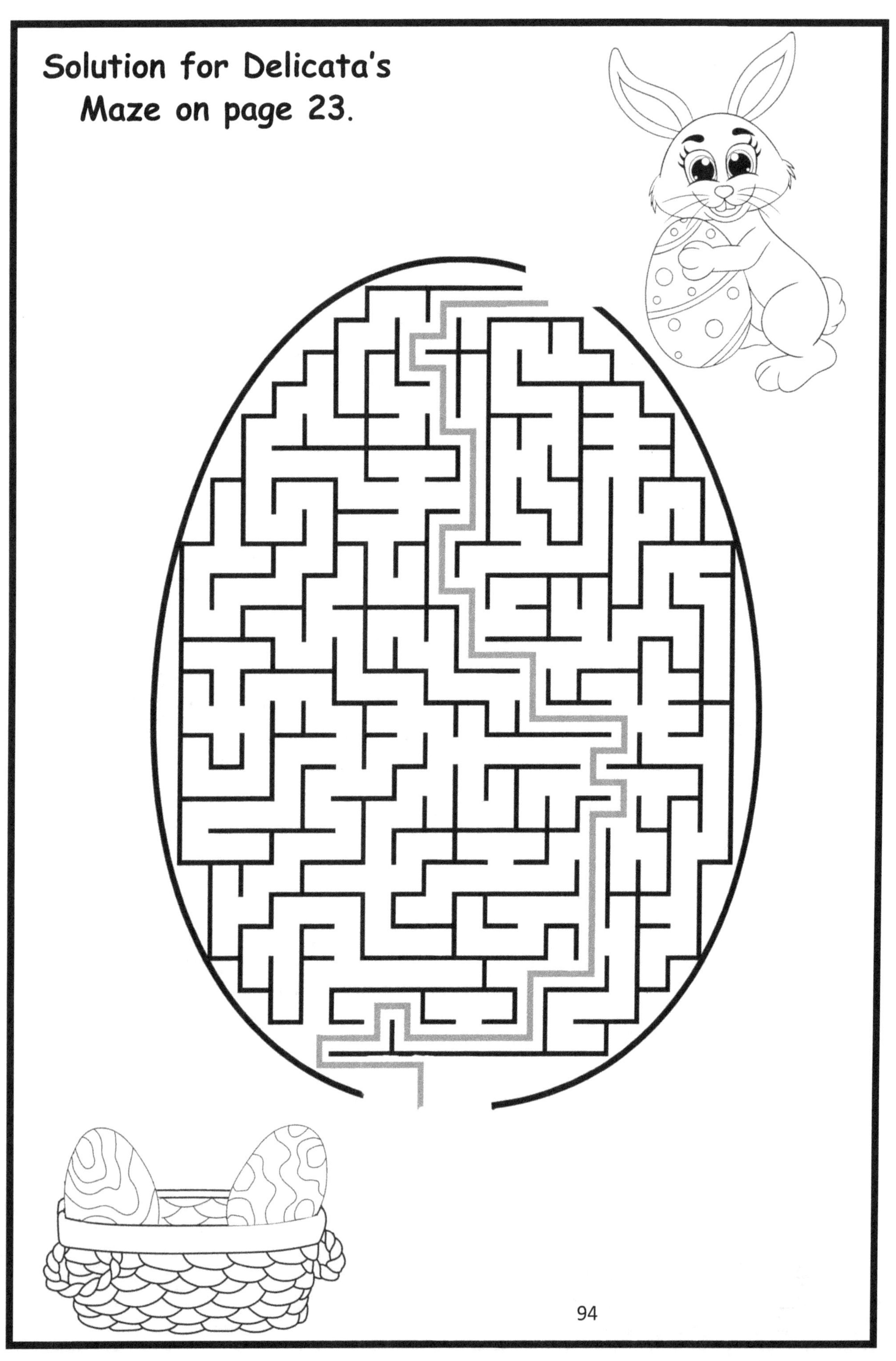

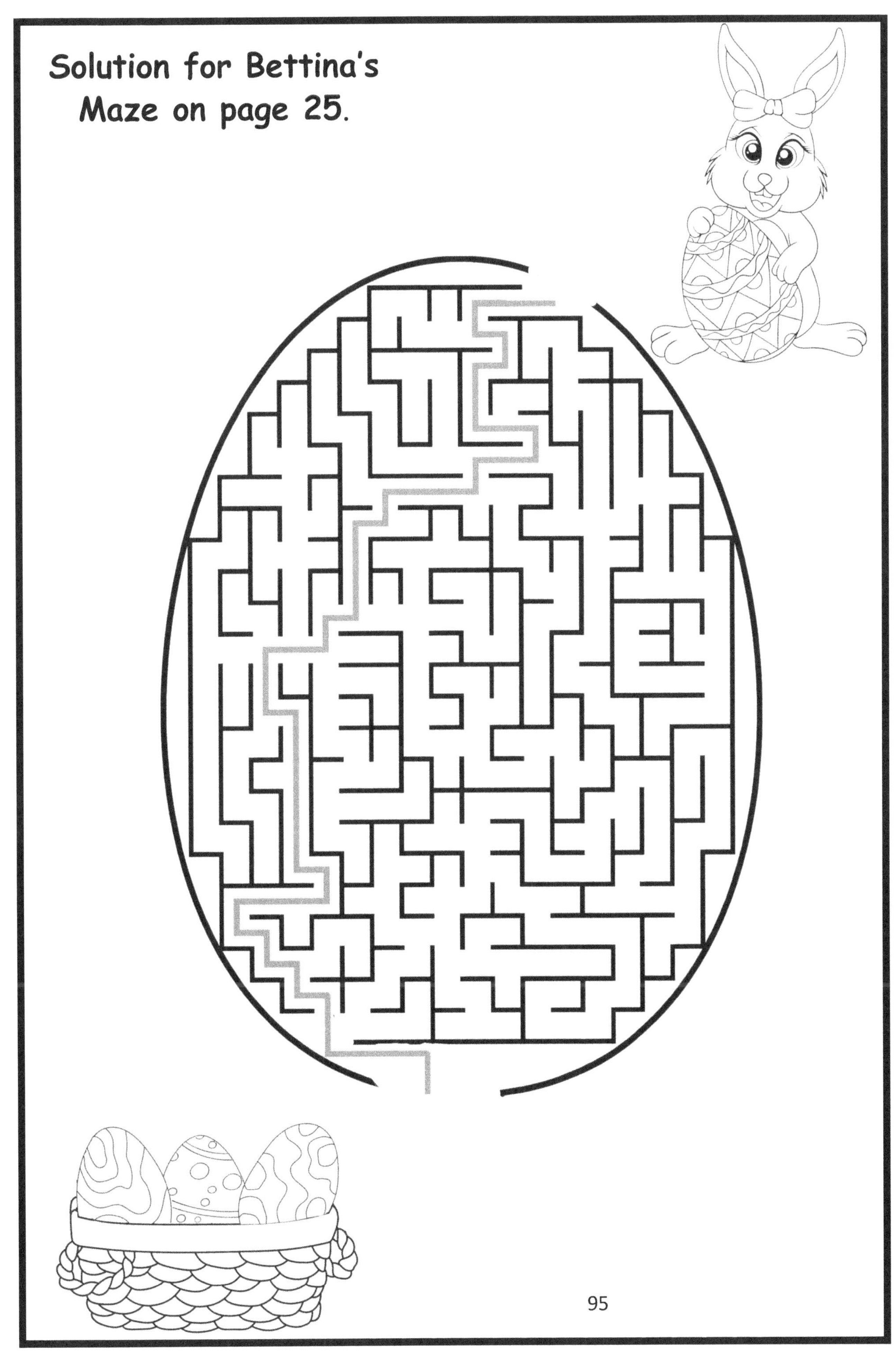

Solution for Bettina's
Maze on page 25.

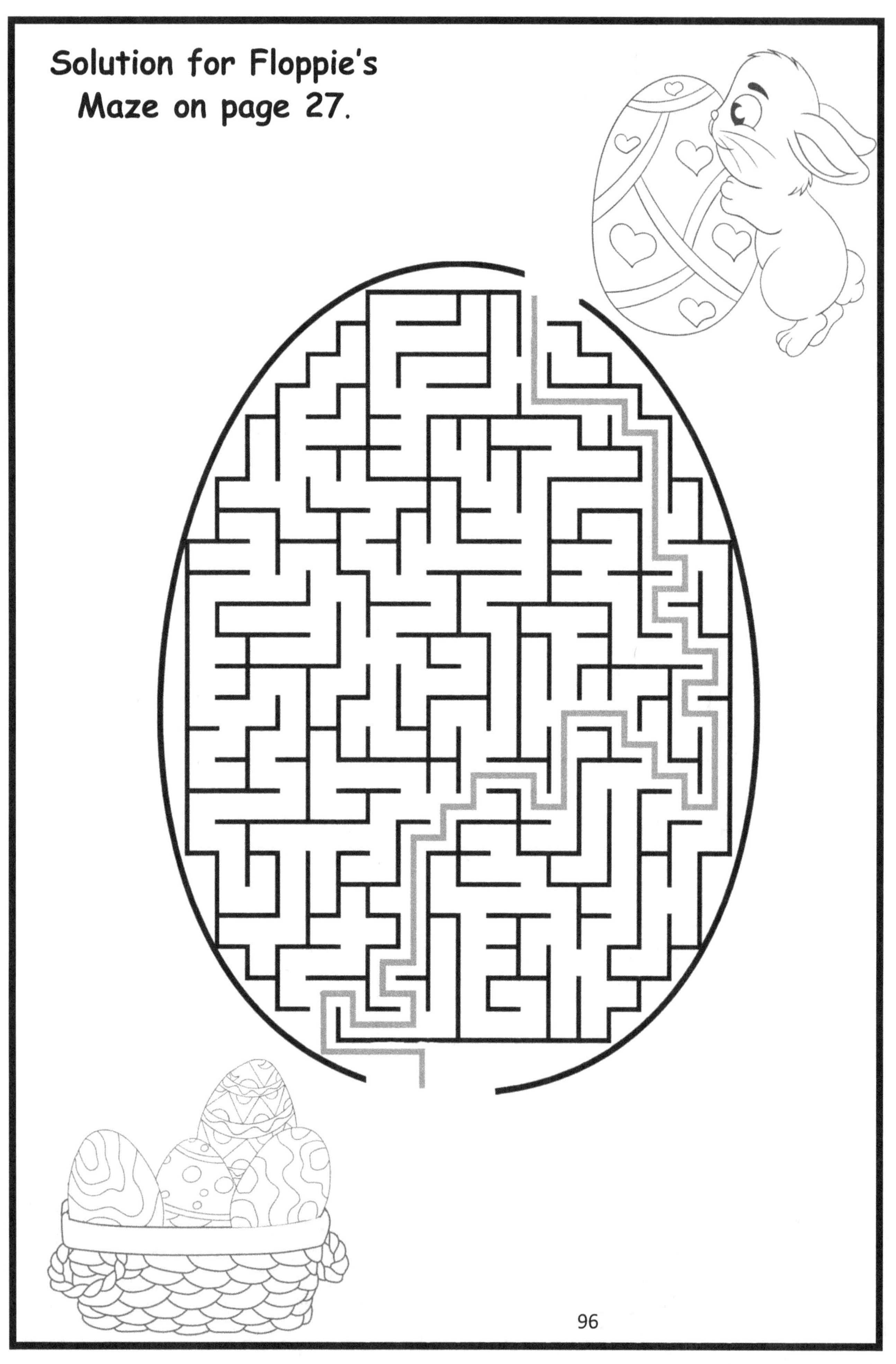

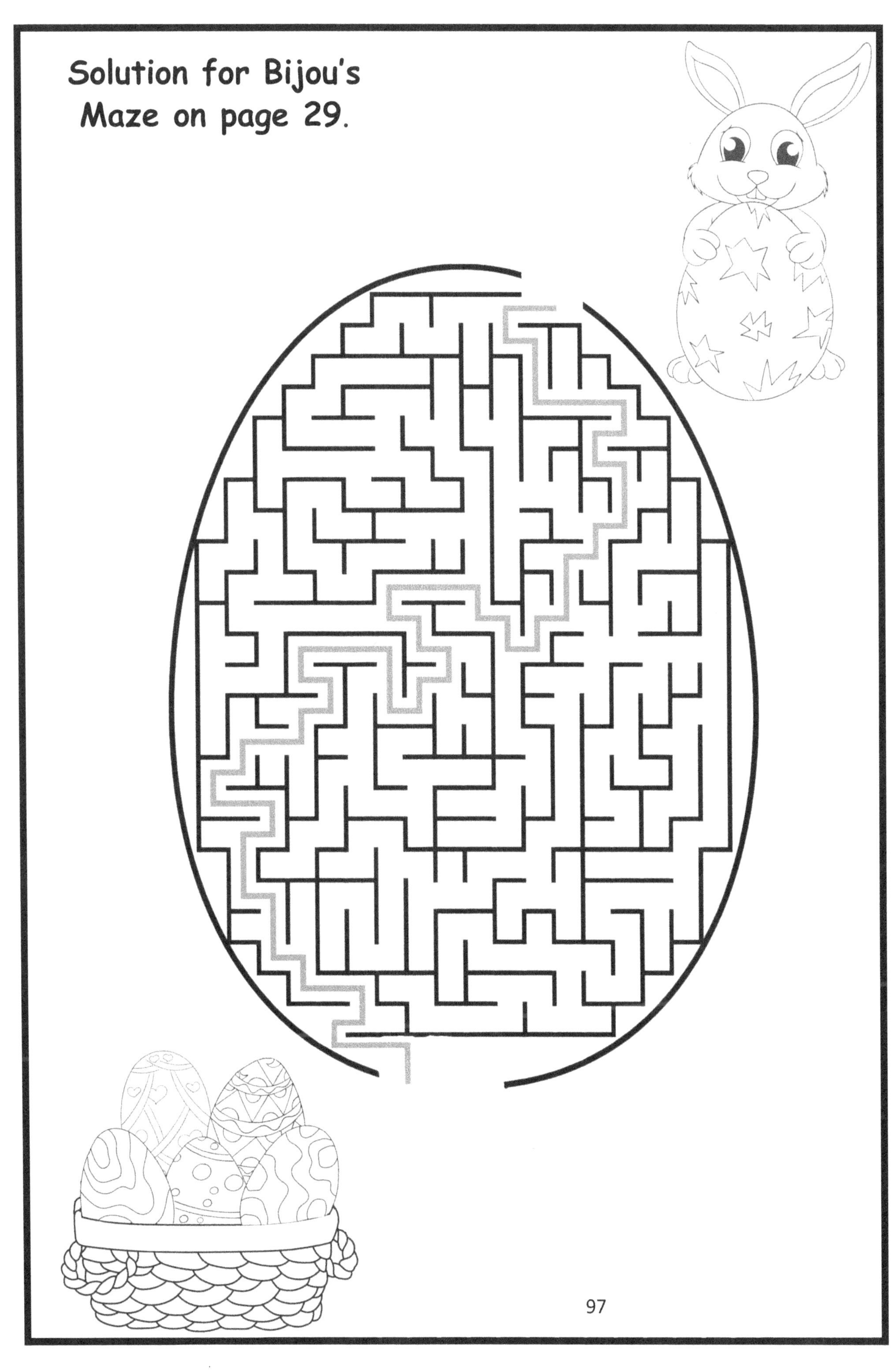

Solution for Bijou's
Maze on page 29.

20 aMAZEing
Squirrely Fun Puzzles

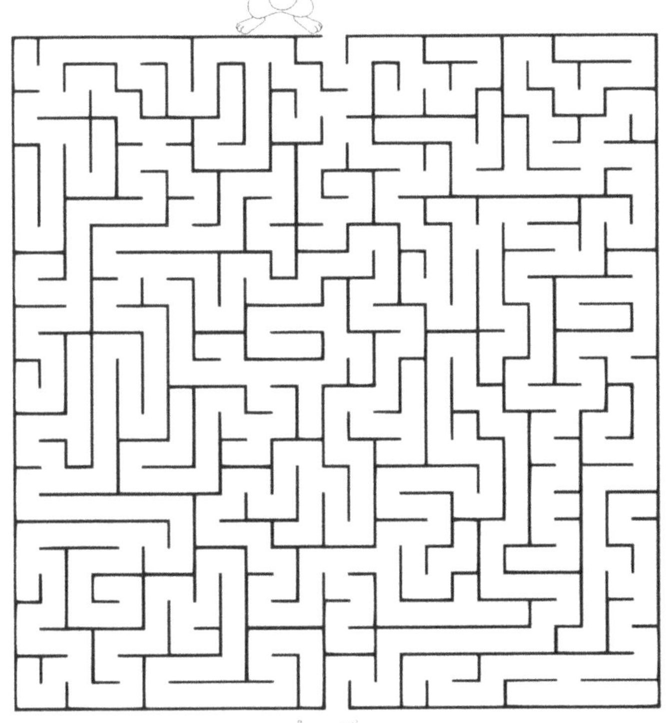

**Cute Chipmunks
and Fun-loving
Squirrels
Need Your Help
to Discover
the Trails to
Where They Store
Acorns for Winter.**

A printable book
of MAZES related to the
"Critter Activity Book"
collection created by
Julia L Wright

HieroGraphics Books

Solution for the Bunny Names
Word Search Puzzle on page 45.

Circle the words in the list when you find them in the square below.

Mark an X next to each word in the list when you find it.

___ BETTINA	___ BRIANNAH	___ HAREBRAIN
___ BEAUFORT	___ BLYTHE	___ SCRUFFY
___ BIGFOOTE	___ DELICATA	___ WHISKAS
___ BIJOU	___ FLOPPIE	___ YODA

Solution for the Bunny Names and Glossary Word Search Puzzle on page 47.

Circle the words in the list when you find them in the square below.

Mark an X next to each word in the list when you find it.

___ BABUK	___ DAVINCI	___ HOPPY
___ BARBRIANA	___ DOZEN	___ MAZE
___ BASKET	___ EGGS	___ POOKIE
___ BUNNY	___ FLOWERS	___ PAMILA
___ BUTTERFLY	___ HEART	___ STARS

		Y	L	F	R	E	T	T	U	B			
									A	U			
									B		N		
		E	Z	A	M				U			N	T
				N		P	O	O	K	I	E	E	Y
		T				A					K	Z	
		R		D	A	V	I	N	C	I	S		O
		A					R		A				D
		E						B					
		H	O	P	P	Y			R				
									S	T	A	R	S
			S								B		
		G		F	L	O	W	E	R	S			
	G												
E													

Solution for the Things You Can Do or Color Word Search Puzzle on page 49.

Circle the words in the list when you find them in the square below.

Mark an X next to each word in the list when you find it.

___ COTTAGE   ___ FLOWERS   ___ MAZE   ___ TULIPS
___ BUNNIES   ___ FOREST   ___ PATH   ___ STARS
___ BASKET   ___ GARDEN   ___ PUZZLES   ___ STUMP
___ BUTTERFLY   ___ HEART   ___ RAINBOW   ___ SUDOKU
___ EGGS   ___ HILL   ___ TREE   ___ WINDOW

						B	U	T	T	E	R	F	L	Y
	C					A	U					O		
F	L	O	W	E	R	S		N	S	T	A	R	S	
	T		T		K		N			E				
	T	R			E			I		S				
	A		H	T	A	P		M	E	T				
	E	G					A	S						
H	E	A		S	E	L	Z	Z	U	P				
		R					E		I					
S		W	O	D	N	I	W			L				
	T			E		U	K	O	D	U	S			
	U			N				T		H				
	M	W	O	B	N	I	A	R			I			
	P				E				L					
	S	G	G	E					L					

Solution for the clues for the Crossword Puzzle where you to had to fill in the name of the Bunny that is described by the clue relating to what they are doing on one of the pages in this book.

ACROSS

1. <u>BABUK</u> is admiring a couple of decorated Easter eggs in his hands.
2. <u>HOPPY</u> is celebrating having gathered five big Easter eggs in his garden.
4. <u>BIGFOOTE</u> needed help to find the path to take one Easter egg to add to an empty basket.
6. <u>BETTINA</u> is wearing a bow between her ears.
7. <u>DAVINCI</u> is painting an egg sitting on a stump in the forest.
9. <u>HAREBRAIN</u> is looking for more eggs among flowers and grass.
11. Beautiful tulips are making <u>BEAUFORT</u> smile.

DOWN

1. Big flowers are making <u>BLYTHE</u> smile.
3. Butterflies flitting from one exotic flower to another are making <u>POOKIE</u> laugh.
4. <u>BARBRIANA</u> is standing under a rainbow.
5. <u>FLOPPIE</u> wants to add an Easter egg decorated with hearts into a basket at the bottom of a maze.
6. Hearts are dancing in the sky above <u>BRIANNAH</u>.
7. <u>DELICATA</u> is holding an Easter egg with circles and stripes to carry to the basket at the bottom of a maze.
8. <u>PAMILA</u> was distracted by tulips, floating hearts and butterflies
10. <u>BIJOU</u> has an Easter egg decorated with stars to fill up a basket at the bottom of a maze.

Solution for the Bunny Names Crossword Puzzle on Page 63.

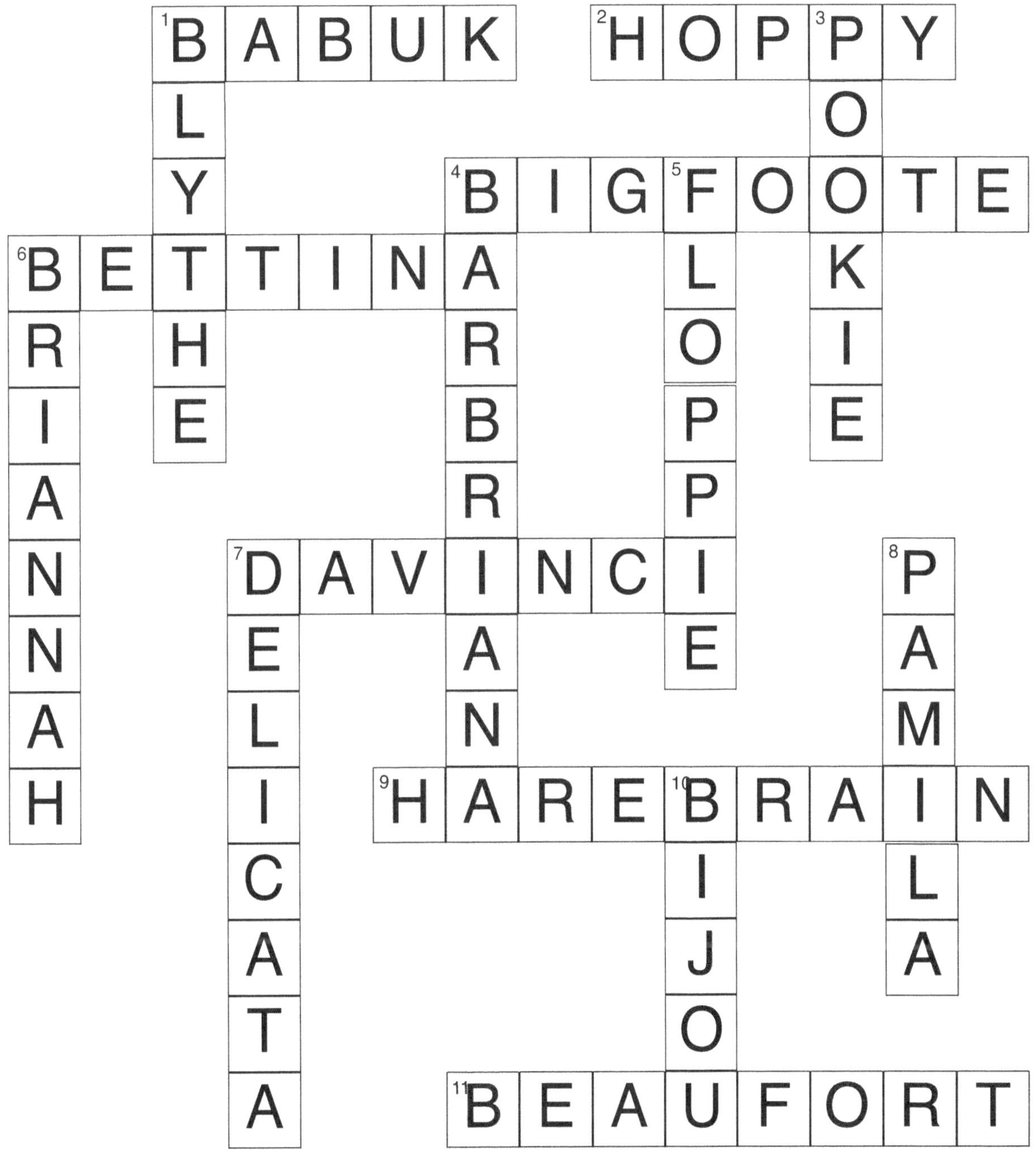

Answers to the Clues for the
Bunny Glossary Words Crossword Puzzle.

ACROSS

1. Barbriana is standing under a <u>RAINBOW</u>.
4. DaVinci is sitting on a <u>STUMP.</u>
5. <u>TWINKLING</u> stars and hearts fill the air above Harebrain.
7. The Bunnies Easter baskets are filled with decorated <u>EGGS</u>.
9. Harebrain wants to get home to <u>HIDE</u> some Easter eggs for his children.
13. <u>TULIPS</u> are in the field that Whiskas will walk past on a path going up a hill.
15. Lovely <u>FLOWERS</u> are blooming in Hoppy's garden.
16. Whiskas is headed to a neighbor's <u>COTTAGE</u> with her Easter basket filled with decorated eggs.
17. There is a <u>BASKET</u> filled with six Easter eggs for you to color on page 31.
18. All the bunnies have <u>DECORATED</u> Easter eggs.

DOWN

2. <u>BUTTERFLIES</u> are distracting Pamila from gathering up four patterned Easter eggs.
3. Butterflies are <u>FLITTING</u> around Babuk.
6. Hoppy has decorated his <u>GARDEN</u> with stars and hearts hanging down on cords.
8. The sky above Blythe is filled with <u>STARS</u> and hearts.
9. <u>HEARTS</u> are joyfully dancing in the sky to welcome Briannah home.
10. Butterflies fly from flower to flower to <u>POLLINATE</u> them.
11. We can see Babuk holding two Easter eggs through a <u>WINDOW</u>.
12. Hoppy took some time to <u>CELEBRATE</u> having four large Easter eggs in his garden.
14. Barbriana has her heart filled with <u>LOVE</u>.

Solution to the Bunny Glossary Words
Crossword Puzzle on page 65.

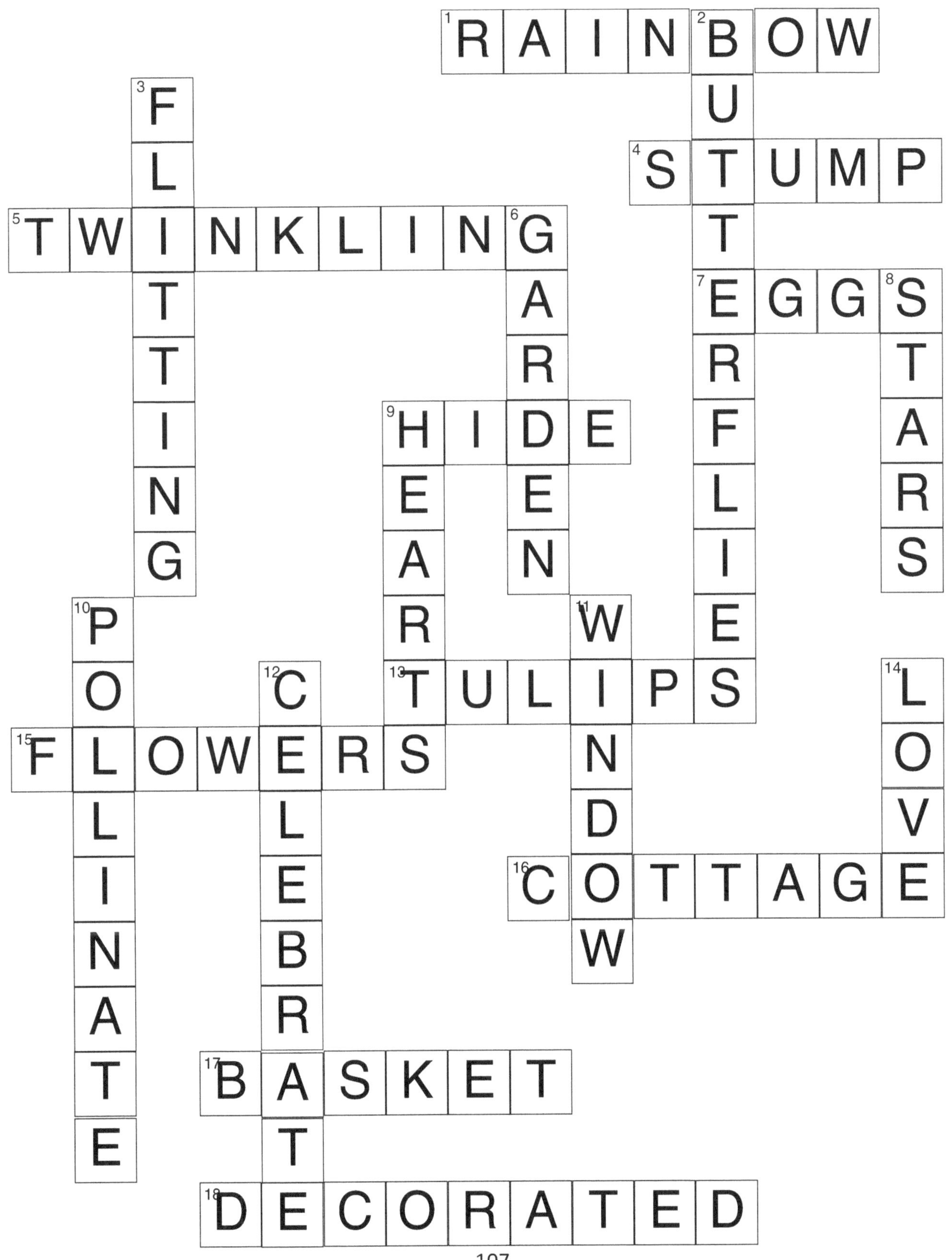

Solution for Eggs, Hearts, Flowers and Stars Sudoku #1 on page 79.

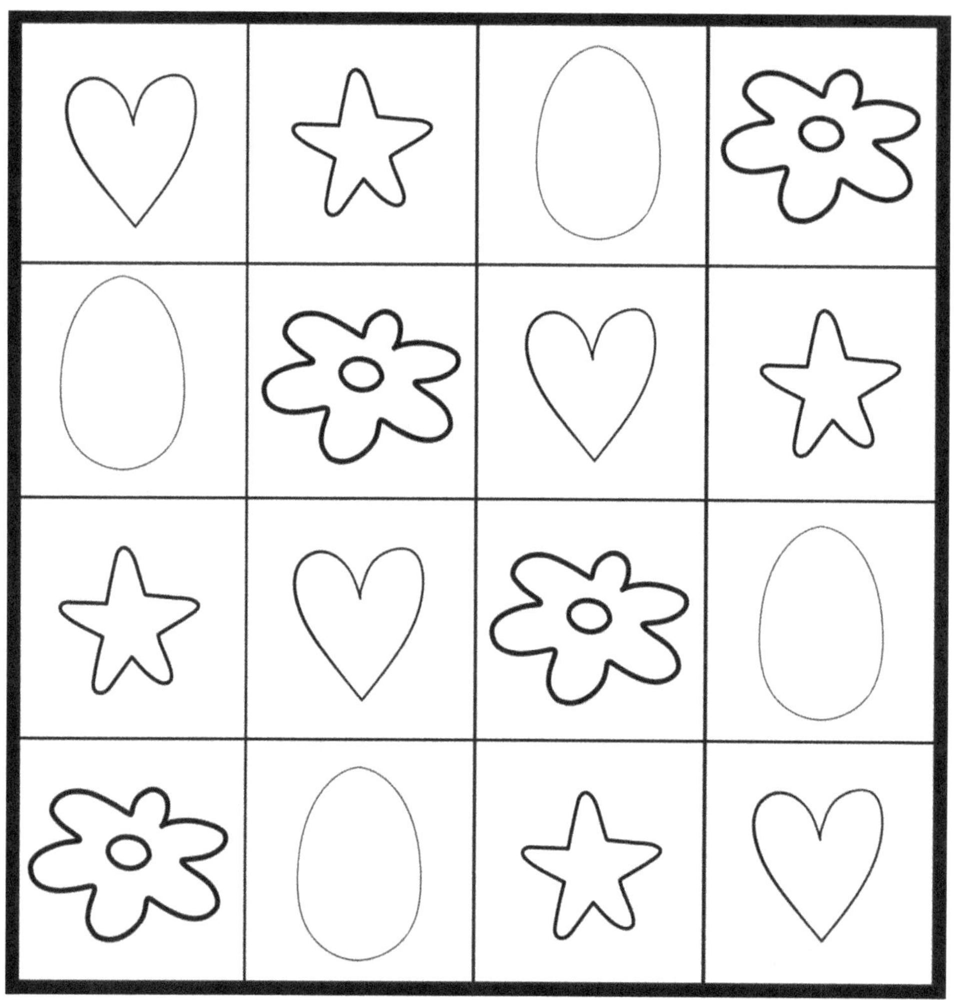

Solution for Eggs, Hearts, Flowers and Stars
Sudoku #2 on page 81.

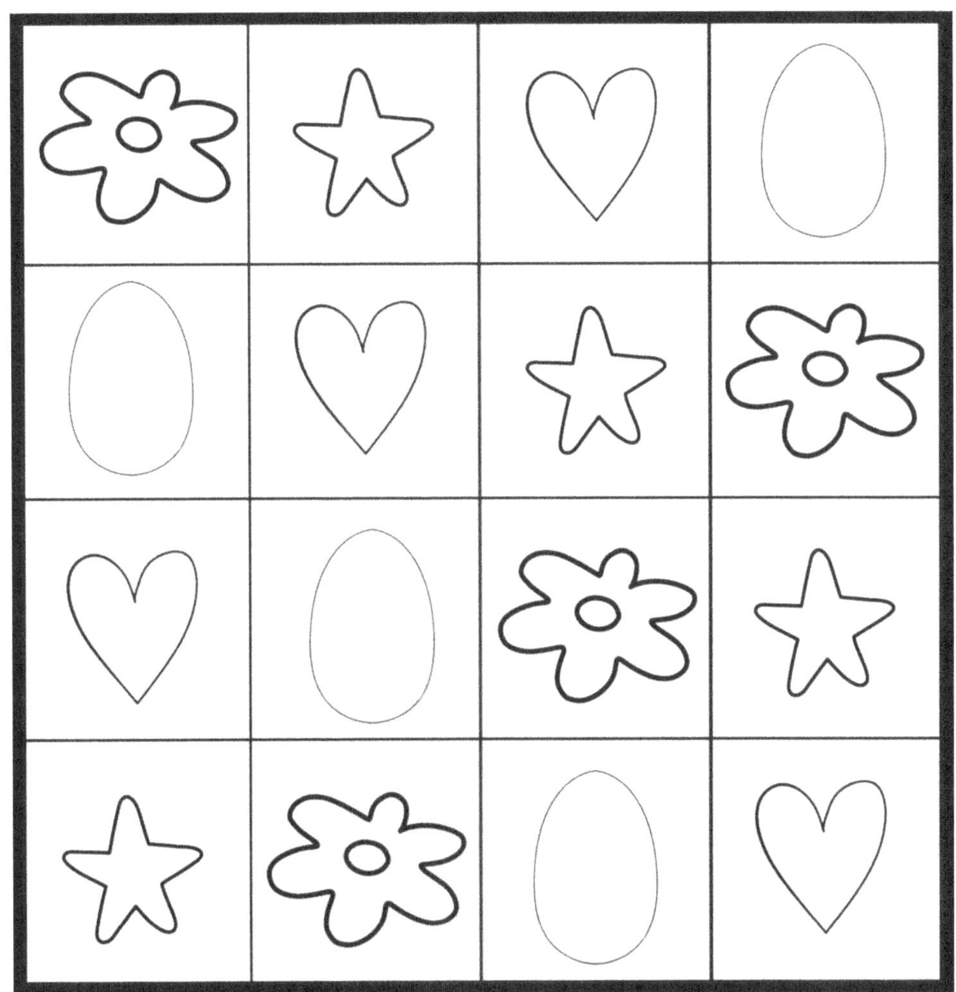

Solution for Eggs, Hearts, Flowers and Stars
Sudoku #3 on page 83.

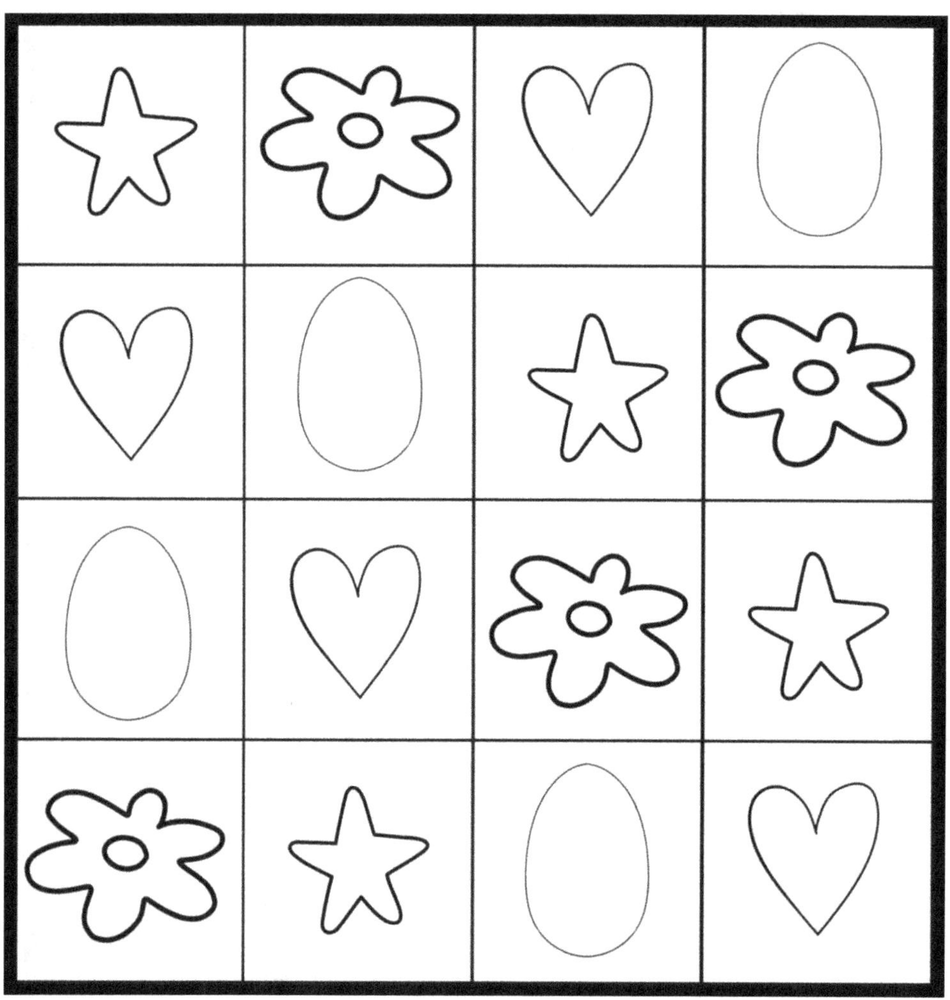

Solution for Eggs, Hearts, Flowers and Stars Sudoku #4 on page 85.

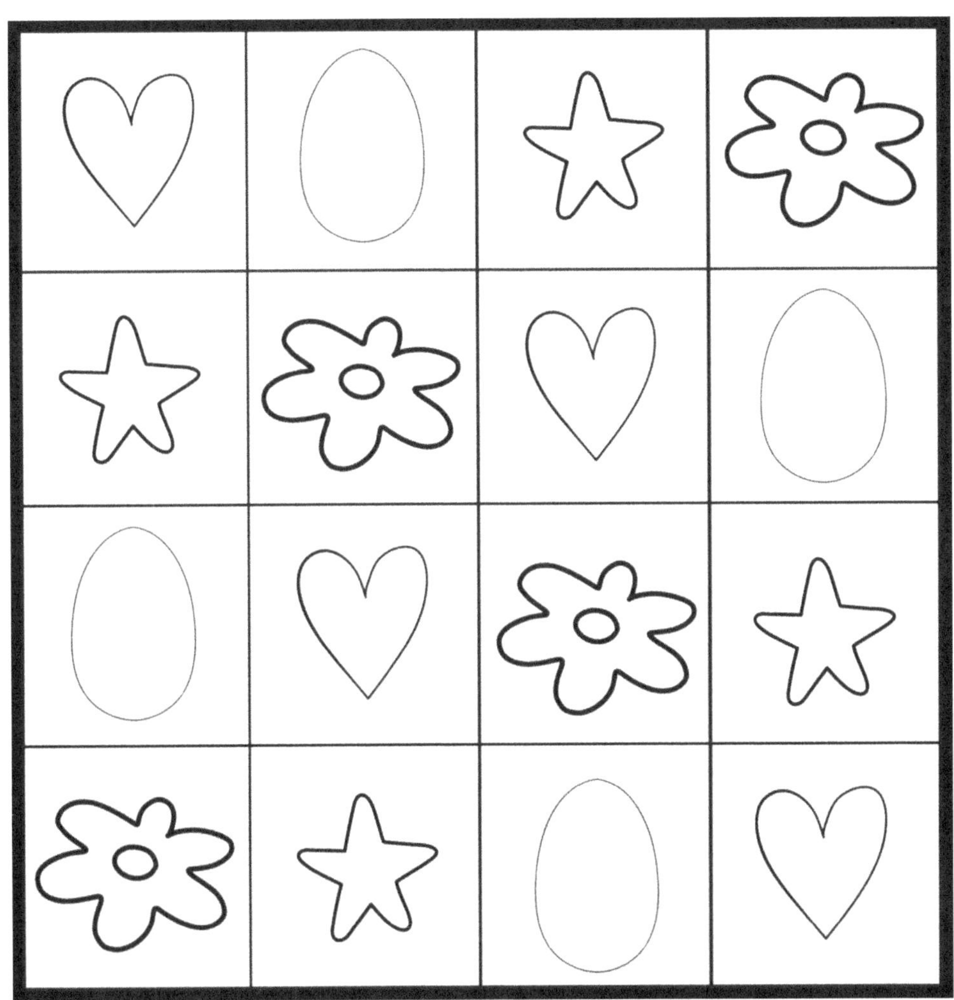

Solution for Eggs, Hearts, Flowers and Stars Sudoku #5 on page 87.

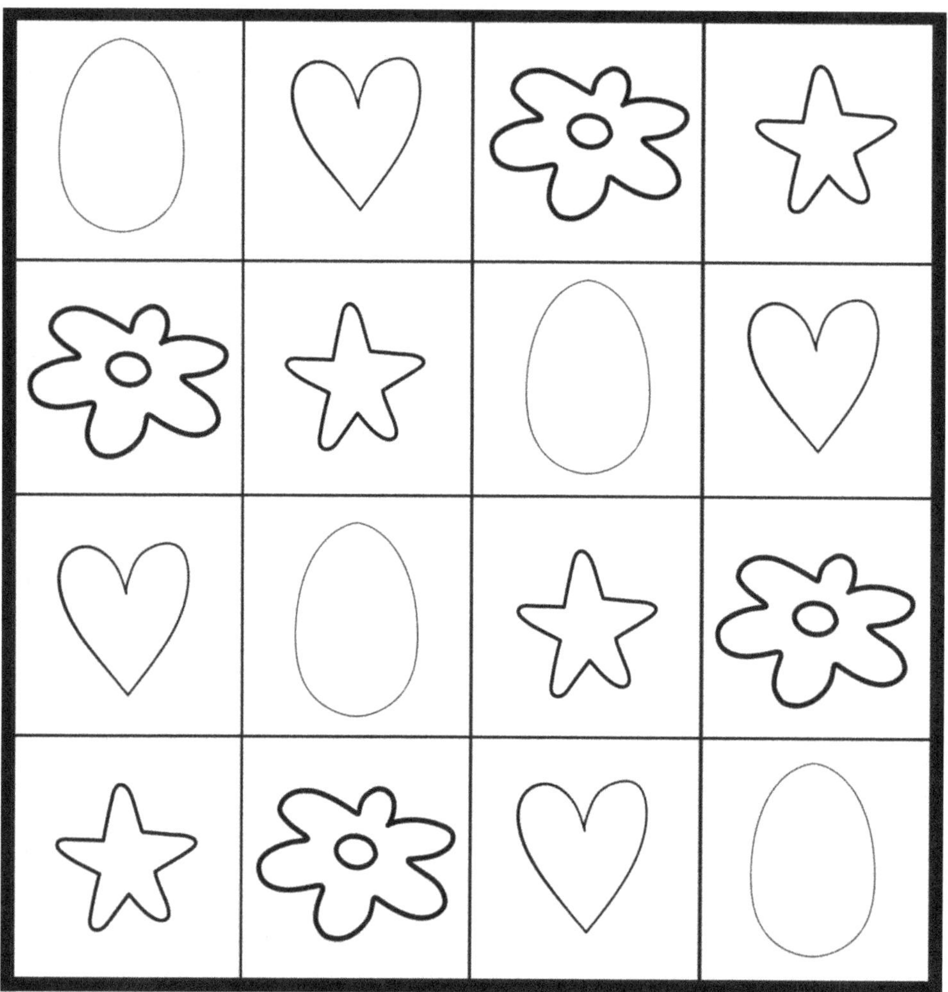

Solution for Eggs, Hearts, Flowers and Stars
Sudoku #6 on page 89.

If you love bunnies, chances are you also enjoy watching squirrels at play. In Violet Burbach's and Julia L. Wright's colorfully illustrated book, "Discover The World Of Squirrels", children can learn interesting facts about these fascinating creatures that live in forests around the world.

This book includes a glossary of new words kids will be introduced to when reading the book.

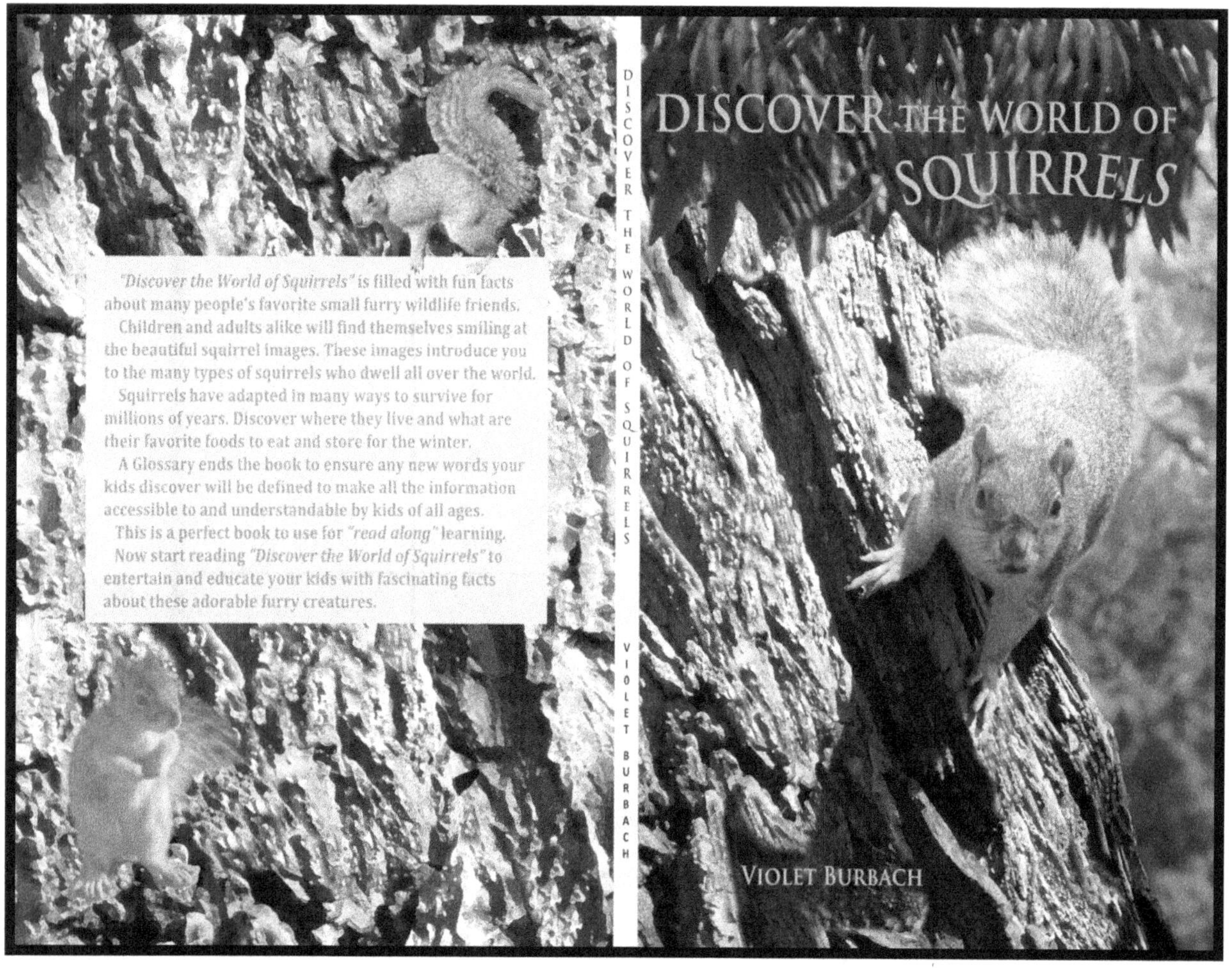

You can find this educational and fun book about squirrels on Amazon at:
https://www.amazon.com/dp/1512255335/

And if you want to learn more about chipmunks and other ground squirrels check out "Discover The World Of Ground Squirrels" at: https://www.amazon.com/dp/0996581634.

Rockey is inviting you to come explore the "Squirrel Coloring And Activity Book" from HieroGraphics Books.

www.amazon.com/dp/0996581669/

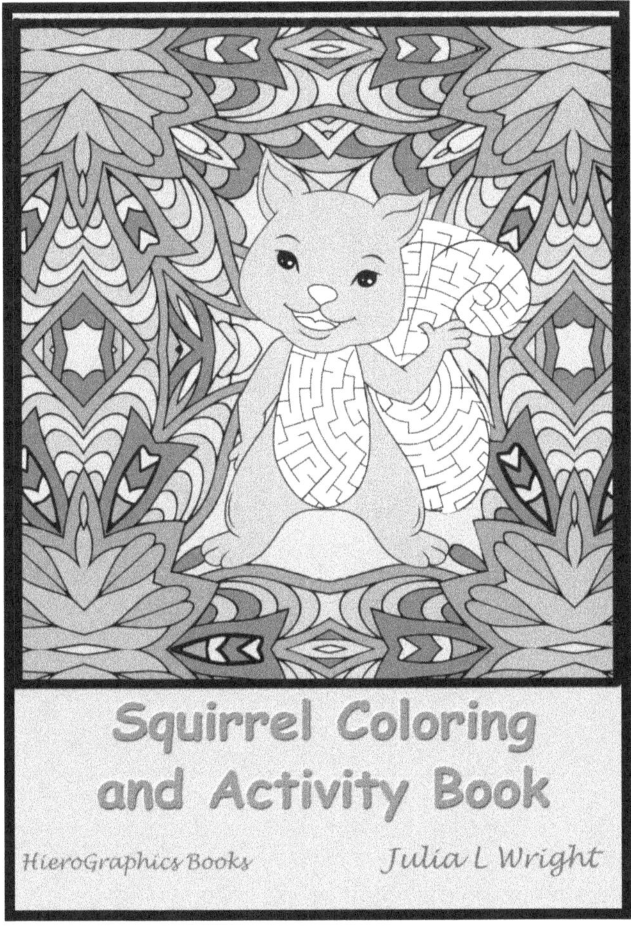

Princess Acorna would like to invite you to come explore the "Chipmunk Coloring And Activity Book" from HieroGraphics Books.

www.amazon.com/dp/0996581650/

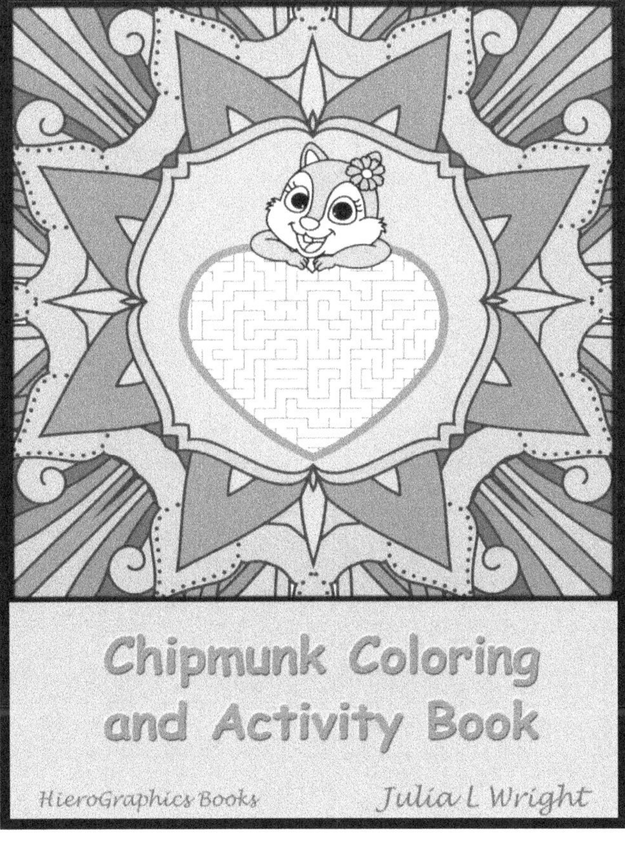

You will find these, and other coloring and activity books created by Julia L. Wright on Amazon.com.

Click on my author name to find more coloring and activities books filled with cute critters and mandalas for hours of fun.

Aspiring artists can use this page to create an image for your story.

Choose a favorite Bunny to write about. Give your story a title using that Bunny's name and what he or she is doing. Have fun telling a story about what this Bunny will do next, starting with the scene on the page you are writing this story about.

TITLE: ____

____

Aspiring artists can use this page to create an image for your story.

Choose a favorite Bunny to write about. Give your story a title using that Bunny's name and what he or she is doing. Have fun telling a story about what this Bunny will do next, starting with the scene on the page you are writing this story about.

TITLE: ____

____

____

____

____

____

____

____

____

____

____

____

____

Aspiring artists can use this page to create an image for your story.

Choose a favorite Bunny to write about. Give your story a title using that Bunny's name and what he or she is doing. Have fun telling a story about what this Bunny will do next, starting with the scene on the page you are writing this story about.

TITLE: ____

Aspiring artists can use this page to create an image for your story.

Choose a favorite Bunny to write about. Give your story a title using that Bunny's name and what he or she is doing. Have fun telling a story about what this Bunny will do next, starting with the scene on the page you are writing this story about.

TITLE: ____

____

____

____

____

____

____

____

____

____

____

____

____

Aspiring artists can use this page to create an image for your story.

Choose a favorite Bunny to write about. Give your story a title using that Bunny's name and what he or she is doing. Have fun telling a story about what this Bunny will do next, starting with the scene on the page you are writing this story about.

TITLE: ____

____

____

____

____

____

____

____

____

____

____

____

____

____

Aspiring artists can use this page to create an image for your story.

Choose a favorite Bunny to write about. Give your story a title using that Bunny's name and what he or she is doing. Have fun telling a story about what this Bunny will do next, starting with the scene on the page you are writing this story about.

TITLE: ____

____

____

____

____

____

____

____

____

____

____

____